Black's Picture Sports

CANOEING

Black's Picture Sports

CANOEING

Alan W. Byde

Adam and Charles Black
London

First published 1978 by A & C Black Ltd
35 Bedford Row, London WC1R 4JH

ISBN 0 7136 1826 4

© Alan W Byde 1978

Byde, Alan
  Canoeing. – (Black's picture sports).
  1. Canoes and canoeing
  I. Title   II. Series
  797.1'22   GV783

ISBN 0-7136-1826-4

Cover and photographs on pages 54 (lower), 66 (lower), 74 Alan Byde; 8, 54 (upper), 66 (upper), 82 Kaija Nyblom

Set and printed in Great Britain by
Page Bros (Norwich) Ltd, Norwich

Contents

1 Introduction

FUN

That's what canoeing should be – fun. But always bear in mind the following three words: safety, discipline and challenge. Remember them in that order, they form the basis of all the advice given in this book.

I asked Bill Davies, senior instructor (sea), British Canoe Union, to act as this book's critic, and he caused me to rethink several sections. He is a swimming teacher too, and is very much against non-swimmers being accepted as novice canoeists. So if you can't swim and you want to canoe, you should really learn how to swim first.

The surf ski is a newcomer to the small craft stable. There is very little in print about these boats, and what there is will almost all be found in the newsletters published by the Surf Lifesaving Association of Great Britain, which have a limited circulation. Bill thought I had overstated their benefits, he knows I design and build them. Maybe I am biased – I re-wrote the section, but I still cannot avoid a hint of admiration for these boats: I like them.

It was suggested that I should include a section on the BCU tests of proficiency. However, these tests do alter in nature from time to time, so I thought it best not to do that. A new series of qualifications is due soon, so my advice to you is to write to the BCU (address on page 93) and find out what the current tests are. You should have little difficulty in passing, if you follow the advice in this book.

In the section on exposure and rescue, I could possibly have included something on resuscitation, both mouth to mouth (or expired air resuscitation, EAR) and chest massage for heart failure. I decided not to do so, as space is limited, and this is a canoeing book primarily. Mind you, if you do take charge of groups of people, be sure you know what to do in such an emergency.

The section on sport has several omissions, notably slalom, long distance racing and sprint. Sailing canoes are important too. The two simple games outlined are there mainly because they are fun games, and it doesn't take a lot of room to introduce them.

I was also asked to include advice on where you should go to start canoeing. There are several way of discovering your nearest canoeing facilities: telephone or call at the appropriate local office of the Sports Council; write to or 'phone the British Canoe Union headquarters in London; seek out your nearest BCU local Canoeing Officer, and most big towns have one nearby; or the local education authority might have some courses available. Best of all your local canoeing club, if you have one, will almost certainly help.

What more can I say? Have fun.

Students from Atlantic College about to go afloat on 1 m-high surf on the Bristol Channel

2 The Craft

There are two main types of craft available in Britain – the canoe and the kayak, although we use the term canoe for both types of craft. The difference between them is that a kayak is propelled by a double-bladed paddle; a canoe by a single-bladed paddle. Strictly speaking, therefore, this book is about kayaking.

BOAT PROFILES

There are three ways in which a three-dimensional object can be described on paper: profile, plan and section. The best way, if space only allows for one, is in profile. The dozen boat profiles (Figure 1A-L on pages 10/11) illustrate the major boat types now in use.

CANOE CHOICE

Choosing your canoe can be a problem. Some clubs will help you to select a good boat but, take it from me, unless the salesman is a keen canoeist himself, you are unlikely to get good advice. He will try and sell you something that suits him, not you. In this short section I cannot examine the ins and outs of each person's requirements, but you should ask yourself the following:

1   What do I/we want it for – playing around in a small area, journeys, surfing, etc.
2   Where will it be used.
3   How much can we spend. The canoe itself is only half

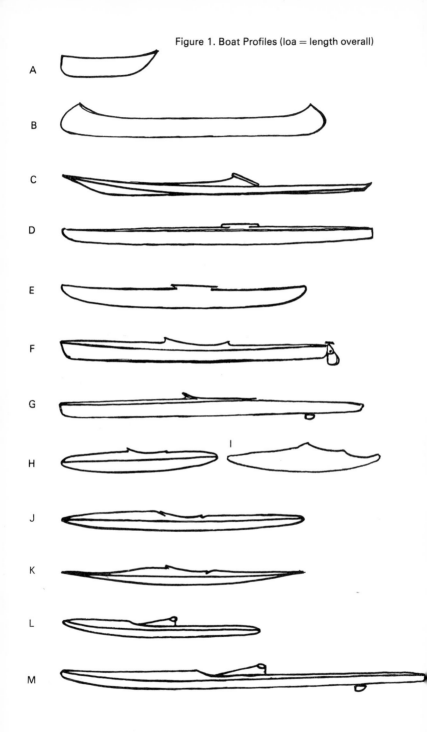

Figure 1. Boat Profiles (loa = length overall)

A The Coracle loa 1.50 m; beam 1.20 m

The Towy fisherman's coracle. The square end is the front, the raised and tapered end the back, in which fish and nets are laid. Other designs still in use are linked with rivers, ie the Severn, Teifi, Taf, Cleddau

B North American Indian Canoe loa 2.45-15.25 m; beam 0.60-2.45 m

The true 'canoe'. The paddler, using a single blade, kneels or sits on a thwart. Some shallow rivers are poled from the standing position

C North Atlantic Eskimo Kayak loa 4.55-6.00 m; beam 0.45-0.70 m

The true 'kayak', or hunter's boat—a floating butcher's bench

D North Pacific Baidarka loa 5.50-6.70 m; beam 0.45-0.66 m

Has only recently gained recognition in the UK as a very seaworthy alternative to the kayak, and has been used on very long sea journeys

E Slalom Canoe loa 4 m; beam 0.70 m (ICF rules)

A very manoeuvrable craft, though bulky by kayak standards. It is decked right over, and can be rolled. The paddler, using a single blade, kneels in the cockpit and is braced in place, thus affording him great flexibility. Used in modern slalom competition and on white water rivers

F Touring Canoe loa 4.55 m approx; beam 0.66 m approx

A typical touring canoe/kayak. It has a large cockpit, and a large capacity for stowing camping equipment. it is moderately fast, and directionally stable, although rudders can be fitted to further assist directional control

G Racing K1 loa 5.20 m; beam 0.51 m (ICF rules)

This conforms to International Canoeing Federation rules for sprint kayaks. It is used for distances of 500 m, 1000 m, 10,000 m and also in long distance competition. It is fitted with an under hull rudder, which provides efficient control, but it is susceptible to damage

H Baths Canoe loa 2.00-3.00 m; 0.50-0.60 m

The 'BAT' – from Baths Advanced Trainer. Many variations on this design are available. It is used for surfing and canoe polo, and is very good for novice training in stroke work and rolling. It is useful on rough mountain streams, but useless for distance work

I Surf Shoe loa 2.45 m approx; beam 0.55-0.60 m

Tiny cockpit and flat bottom, the weight is well aft of centre, for good planing ride on a wave. Sharp 'rails' where sides meet bottom, for speed

J Slalom Kayak loa 4.00 m: beam 0.60 m

An old style craft, often used now for general purposes, and for touring. A highly manoeuvrable craft, which is lively in rough water, but not much good for distance paddling. It is often used on surf, and is also a good novice training craft. A good first buy for the average novice

K Slalom Kayak loa 4.00 m; 0.60 m

The latest style of slalom kayak. The ends, being pointed and lacking in buoyancy, dive easily under the poles or gates in slalom competition. However, the use of such a craft could prove dangerous to others, and I should have to complain to the paddler, if I saw one being surfed on a busy beach. But, for its purpose, within the rules, it is an ideal craft

L Rescue Ski loa 3.65 m; beam 0.55 m

A newcomer to surf paddling. Originally used as a craft for rescue in surf, there is no spray deck to fix, so it is impossible to be trapped, even in a wrecked boat. This craft is controlled by the competition rules of the Surf Lifesaving Association of Great Britain. It is also a very good craft for novices – a sort of surf BAT

M Competition Ski loa 6.00 m max; beam 0.55 m

Developed from Australian and South African lifeguard designs as a racing craft, this is a sort of sea-going K1. It is subject to the rules of the SLSA of GB, and has the same open cockpit as the rescue ski the cost – equipment, lifejackets etc will also be required.

4 Is young John likely to lose interest after a few weeks. If so, does it have a good resale value.
5 Do I buy new or second hand.
6 What about maintenance.
7 How heavy is it. Can I carry it.
8 Is it too light. Will it be weak.
   And so on and so on.

If you see a second hand canoe for sale, you should consider it methodically. A good vendor will go through these points for you, but it's better to make sure yourself.

1 Press with your hand on each side of the upturned hull, just in front of and just behind the cockpit. A cracked hull, still watertight but now weakened, will show a distinct edge where flexion cracks are developing. (Do this on ground where the deck will not be scratched or damaged.)
2 Turn the canoe right way up, and press down hard just in front of and just behind the cockpit. The foredeck should bear the weight of an upturned waterlogged canoe in a deep water rescue. The rear

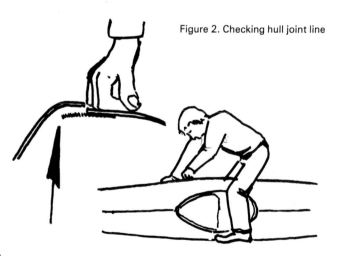

Figure 2. Checking hull joint line

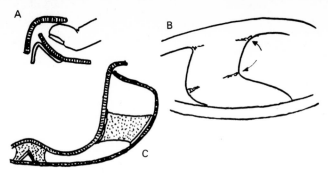

Figure 3. A checking cockpit rim; B flexion cracking on seat; C seat braces

deck should bear your weight when you climb in. Try getting in.

3   Stand astride the canoe on its edge (Figure 2). Press down all round one side of the hull side of the joint line. If the joint is sprung, the canoe will flex, leak and sink. This sort of damage isn't always visible. It can be repaired – when you know what to do.

4   Lift the cockpit rim quite strongly all round with your forefinger (Figure 3A). If it is loosened, it is not easy to cure. If the canoe has no cockpit rim, refuse it – or you're in for trouble. Is there room to tuck a spray deck under the rim.

5   Does the seat have flexion cracking, due to seat sway, on the side flanges where they meet the seat and rim (Figure 3B). If so, the seat stays are broken or were never installed. The seat should be substantial, about 4 mm thick.

6   Run your finger under the cockpit rim where your knees go. Rough edges or spiky bits of resin will irritate and chafe. The rim joint should be filled with smooth filler.

7   Run your hand behind the side of the seat (Figure 3C). Are the braces firmly fixed? In a second hand canoe, the single brace under the seat will almost certainly be broken. A brace there is simple to fix, but it is hit hard in use when bouncing over shallows.

8   Look at the front and rear keel lines of the hull. Are they chafed through or nearly through. I build in extra thickness here to protect the boat against wear, but not every builder does.

9   The seat may be pressing down inside on the bottom of the hull. Typically a flat bottomed canoe will flex upwards against the seat, and so constant wear will generate a hole – in the seat pan, too.

10 Look at the general condition of the canoe. Is the joint trim done in a resin strip, or a tatty tape leaving the unsealed joint showing. An unsealed joint allows the wet in; a resin-sealed joint, even if untidy and damaged, is better than a taped one.

11 Is there a footrest fitted. Is it fail safe. Does it undo and adjust as it should, or are all the bolts corroded solid.

12 Are the buoyancy blocks, air bags, etc sound. Remember you can always stuff a partly inflated car inner tube into each end to provide buoyancy for the canoe. Tie them in place.

13 Are there deck lines fitted. Is there a pair of toggles, one at each end. Is there a paddle park.

In short, your check list reads:
1   Flexion – of the deck, cockpit and hull.
2   Wear – at each end.
3   Joint breaks – each side; and the joint trim.
4   Cockpit rim.
5   Seat stays.
6   Deck fittings.
7   Fail-safe footrest.
8   Buoyancy complete.

THE CANADIAN CANOE

The Canadian canoe was originally built from birch bark, with an internal stiffening of wooden laths and frames, and was not decked. The modern Canadian canoe is built from glass reinforced plastic – grp. The

14

paddler (sealed with a spray deck) kneels inside a small cockpit made in the totally enclosed deck.

The paddling stroke in the Canadian canoe takes place *only* on one side. Kneel in the boat, or practice on a bank where you can get the blade deep into the water without falling in yourself. Hold the paddle as shown in Figure 4. As you drive the paddle along, when your lower hand is level with your hip, flick your upper hand over so that the blade is now slicing the water. Press outwards with the blade at the end of the stroke. This outward pressure takes place every stroke with the touring canoe, but the slalom paddler takes several short sharp digs with the blade, then uses one stroke for correction. Your top hand can turn either inwards or outwards for correction.

Figure 4. Correct grip for single blade paddle

SURF SKI

This type of craft has been developed quite recently in Britain. The solo competition skis are becoming very similar to K1s, but are longer and more stable. The solo rescue ski is small, and is really a surfing baths boat. The double ski is not yet so refined for speed, and will probably never approach that of the K2.

Compared with the kayak, the ski has certain advantages in surf and some disadvantages. The cockpit is open, with hollows for the seat and feet. There is a 'tree' between the knees which allows the paddler to hold on in rough water. There is no spray deck to adjust or become faulty. The footrest is in the open and adjustment is very easy. No fail safe system is required, because there is no deck over the legs to collapse and trap the paddler (Figure 5).

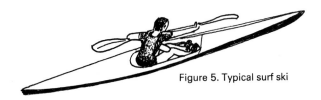

Figure 5. Typical surf ski

There is a psychological advantage in using this craft for your first capsize – you are free to leave the craft simply by releasing the grip of your thighs on the tree. The same sense of being trapped is removed in rolling drills also, thus removing some of the mental tension.

There are drawbacks. One is that the boat is a totally enclosed 'pod', and drain bungs are provided. Grp materials do not suffer from rot; however, being totally enclosed, the ski contains air at normal air pressure when it leaves the beach. As soon as it is plunged into rough water, the pressure outside increases above the pressure inside the craft. This causes the area suffering from a pressure difference to distort. The ski is never waterlogged, unless torn open by severe turbulence.

One final drawback that would bother some kayak handlers is that the seat hole and feet recesses hold water, and the added weight must slow the ski down a little. The extra weight would be no more than 4.5 litres – 4.5 kg, but that is quarter the weight again of a surfing kayak or ski.

3 The Canoeist

CLOTHING

I've tried many ways of protecting myself from the loss of bodily heat; the one I recommend is not expensive – and it does work. Cold weather wear is given here – which is needed 10 months out of every year in Britain. Canoeing in warmer climates will alter your requirements.

1. Swimming clothes underneath.
2. Cotton long sleeved vest, ie rugby shirt, or 'long john' type vest.
3. Wool socks, or neoprene socks attached to boots (divers type).

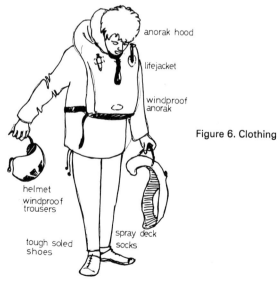

Figure 6. Clothing

anorak hood

lifejacket

windproof anorak

helmet
windproof trousers

tough soled shoes

spray deck socks

4   Lined neoprene, 3 mm or 4 mm wet suit trousers, of the long john type. Note that the vest top must be well cut away around the pectoral (chest) muscles and under the armpits. Chafing can ruin a good day's canoeing.

5   One, or even two, woollen sweaters, one with a roll neck.

6   Windproof anorak, of the proofed nylon type. It *must not* be of the quilted cotton type. The anorak should have a hood which can be pulled close around the face, to protect you from driving spray, rain etc.

7   A woollen hat which can be pulled down over the ears is a very good idea – about one third of bodily heat loss is from the head, neck and shoulders.

8   A lifejacket, apart from affording personal buoyancy, can also enhance heat insulation for the body. The BSS 3595 does not protect the back from heat loss. A buoyancy waistcoat with closed cell foam ribs all round is good for heat and impact protection, but not so good in maintaining body posture when in the water.

9   Spray deck if you are using a kayak or canoe.

10 Helmet to protect your head from impact.

11 Windproof trousers, made of proofed nylon, if you intend walking about a great deal in a strong breeze.

12 Tough rubber soles to protect your feet.

13 Avoid tight collars, they cause headaches.

Canoeist's Helmet This must be worn to protect your head from low velocity impact with sharp objects like rocks, other canoes and paddles, and the sand bottom when surfing. It is also required by the rules in slalom, white water racing, surfing competition, and canoe polo. It must be lightweight, and have holes in it to let out the water when rolling. It should be colourful (red, orange or yellow preferably) to assist rescue in an accident at sea. The chin strap should fit under the chin, but the strap does chafe on long voyages. Chin strap fastening is always a problem, but moulded chin cups are not

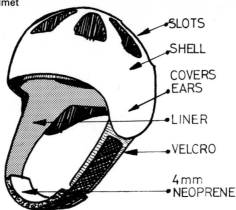

Figure 7. Canoeist's helmet

SLOTS

SHELL

COVERS EARS

LINER

VELCRO

4mm NEOPRENE

recommended, since their rigid rims can cause painful pressure points. The best system I have seen is a 'Velcro' touch fastener fixed at one side (Figure 7), or a stretchy elastic webbing strap.

LIFEJACKETS AND BUOYANCY AIDS

The British Standard Specification (BSS) is satisfied by some lifejackets which are not suitable for use by canoeists. Other buoyancy aids which do not satisfy the BSS however clearly satisfy canoeists' requirements.

The average white water canoeist, and probably a surfer too, would not wear a BSS 3595 lifejacket. It is most likely that if he did he would run into trouble when attempting to punch out through big waves. Nevertheless he knows that it is helpful to have some – but not too much – buoyancy. He may consider that the buoyancy of the foam neoprene wet suit is sufficient; I do not find this is enough for me, and I use a buoyancy waistcoat.

The two main types of personal buoyancy aid are illustrated in Figure 8. A is the lifejacket which satisfies BSS 3595 only when inflated, and B the buoyancy waistcoat which never satisfies BSS 3595. The BSS 3595 lifejacket can be obtained in various different styles, but

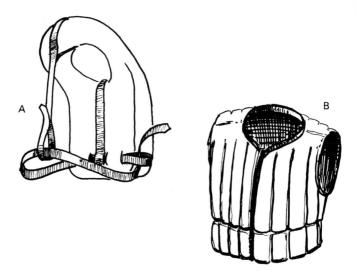

Figure 8. A BSS 3595 lifejacket; B waistcoat buoyancy aid

the type suitable for the sailor is likely to be wide and thin across the chest, and is thus not suitable for the canoeist because the wide air bag chafes the arms and restricts cross-body movement. However, all types have the same basic chest mounted air bag and neck piece, with a webbing harness tied at the side and lifting becket. Various buckles have been used, but the simple knot is best – if you know how to tie it. Novices can make a mess of the straps, and unless the person in charge checks it thoroughly, the lifejacket can be worse than useless. If you are on your own, read the instructions and check that the lifejacket is properly adjusted as follows:

1   Put your hand under the front lower part of the life-jacket.
2   Lift that hand. If the lifejacket top comes up and covers your nose, the waist strap is not tight enough.
3   Take hold of both sides of the lifejacket. Pull to one side, then the other. If it moves more than 5 cm it isn't right

One way to fasten the waist strap for the BSS 3595 life-jacket is shown in Figure 9. Some straps may have buckles which corrode and jam, and don't hold under tension when wet. It is then necessary to lock these with a knot similar to the one shown. You may pull the tail through as a bow, for easy release. However, it might just release easily as you are paddling – and you won't know. You capsize, and the lifejacket is easy to find – but where, dear paddler, are you? You may have gathered that my opinion of the BSS 3595 lifejacket is not high.

Figure 9. Waist strap fastening

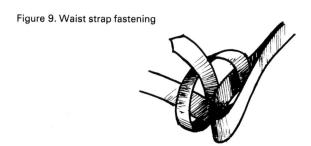

The buoyancy waistcoast is not expensive and it is simple – although zips can jam. Provided that it is the right size it is automatically adjusted laterally and vertically when you put it on. There is no inflatable stage, therefore no inflator valve to give trouble. No air bag to puncture, therefore no leaks. The padding provides thermal insulation and impact cushioning, which the BSS 3595 lifejacket does not. The bouyancy waistcoat won't float you right way up if you're unconscious, but for general reliability and simplicity, it's what I want for me. I have had the same one since 1970; few BSS 3595 lifejackets last that long without some maintenance, and even then only if they are fitted with a cover to reduce chafing of the corners when in use.

If you are to be responsible for other people, buy BSS 3595; not to protect your charges so much as to provide reliable professional protection for yourself if ever, perish the thought, you should have a fatality to deal with in court. If you are buying for yourself, then what I have written here is based on 19 years of active canoeing in all kinds of conditions, and I have swung from all-out acceptance of the BSS 3595 and advocacy of its use, to a preference for a buoyancy waistcoat. Use whichever you like, but be certain of the reasons for your choice.

MUSCLE GROUPS

Paddling will develop certain muscle groups, which implies aching muscles until they are fit to do the work demanded of them. It will help if you know what to expect, and how to reduce the ache.

On your first outing, you will probably sit facing squarely forwards and use only your arms to push the paddle. With your wrists locked, and your fists gripped tight on the shaft, your arms will remain bent at the elbows. In this uncomfortable and soon painful posture, all the strain is concentrated on the muscles in your upper arm, neck, and across the top of the back of your shoulders. To correct this:

1   Relax your hand grip every time you push forwards. This allows your wrist to unlock, and your elbow to straighten.
2   With your now straightened arm pushing forwards at eye level, the stroke can be lengthened and strengthened by pushing forwards with your shoulder.

Once you use your arms properly, you will start to use your shoulders, which in turn will start the thin sheets of muscle across the belly and ribs working. Now your rib muscles will ache, especially where the lower rib lies. This is good, but your action still has some faults, since all the movement is taking place above a rigidly fixed pelvis.

What you must now do is free your hips for action. If you are in a slalom type of kayak relax your knees, except in rough water. More open types of cockpit allow more ease around the hips, but it is more difficult to stay in the cockpit in rough conditions. With your knees relaxed, your legs can be 'pedalled'. Racing practice states – right arm forwards as left leg straightens. However, I have found that when I must paddle hard, my right leg straightens when my right arm is going forwards. This way I think I can extend the stride of the paddle by putting it into the water just a little further forwards. However you will have to decide yourself on the best method for you.

With this easing of the knees, your hips can now swivel, and your toes press against the foot bar alternately. This puts pressure on the calf, upper thigh and under thigh muscles – with all this powerful muscle being brought into use, something happens, and this is shown by the boat going faster through the water. Unless you are a racing paddler, this sort of action requires active thought and constant practice. But it is only through that sort of self discipline that efficient action can be developed.

Four points to remember:

1   Sit up.
2   Swing your shoulders.
3   Use your legs.
4   Reach high with your upper elbow.

LAND CONDITIONING

One ache that is inevitable with a kayak sitting position is an ache in the belly muscles – another is an ache in the groin. These will pass after the first hour or two, provided you keep in practice. To enjoy this passing of the ache in comfort, sit on a cushion in front of the TV (say) at a suitable distance. Place your feet against a solid object, like a stool, or a chair, or a dog. Lean slightly forwards. Watch TV for two hours.

Find an open space, and take with you a 1.50 m pole, or your paddle. Place the pole over your shoulders like a yoke, your arms over the pole, your hands extended towards the ends. Select a mark on a straight line in front of you. Lean forwards. Bend your knees and hips. Perch on your toes. Now the muscle tensions are similar to those you will experience when sitting in a kayak. Swing one hand across the mark, return and swing your other hand across the mark. Your shoulders are now turning through 180°. Drive from your toes. Try and swing at 60 to the minute, then build up to 50 swings in 30 seconds. Return to an easy swing. Sprint and stroll, sprint and stroll. If you keep it up for more than 5 minutes to start with, it will be unusual. You stay on the spot of course.

Flexibility of arm movement is a good thing. Try this. Take the paddle or pole in a wide overhand grip, hands about 1.50 m apart. Stand up straight. Put the pole across to the right side, the pole should be quite vertical. Lower your left arm behind your back, until the pole is horizontal, with both arms straight at the elbows, and hands reversed grip. Swing your right arm up and over your head until the pole is vertical at your left shoulder. Your hands do not shift their grip at any time. It isn't easy at first, and you will probably drop the pole, but try it. I find it quite enjoyable just before going afloat, a sort of winding up. Try to reverse the direction of rotation. It's a good exercise in muscle control.

4 The Canoe's Equipment

BUOYANCY

The buoyancy of a canoe is of two different types. Inherent buoyancy, that which the canoe derives from displacing water; and applied buoyancy, the buoyancy put inside the canoe so that when it is waterlogged, it can still remain afloat.

There are various way of 'applying' buoyancy inside a canoe.

1   A built-in polystyrene block, which performs the dual function of affording buoyancy to a swamped hull, and affording support between the deck and the hull, a necessary extra source of strength in a lightweight boat.
2   Two part resin foam (polyurethane), which is mixed outside the boat and poured into the ends of the canoe, where it foams up to thirty times its liquid volume and sets firm within ten minutes. It absorbs water in use, and therefore loosens.
3   Air bags made of PVC material with inflation tubes can be used. Sometimes these bags contain a loose block of polystyrene, so that even if the bags deflate, there is always a reserve of buoyancy. However, since these bags are out of sight they are usually out of mind, and unless they are looked after carefully, they will often be found to be deflated.
4   Air tanks formed with sealed bulkheads are a good idea for deep water boats, but are useless in shallow water craft. The bulkheads make rigid sections in the hull, and when an obstruction strikes the hull, the

stresses and eventual breaks are found to concentrate where the bulkhead is fixed.

I prefer to use the pillar block of polystyrene in a shallow water boat, and the air tank bulkhead method in a deep water kayak (Figure 10). The surf ski is a fully enclosed unit. Tiny leaks do occur through the joints, and so a drain plug is required.

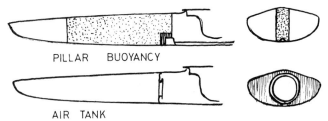

PILLAR   BUOYANCY

AIR   TANK

Figure 10. Pillar buoyancy (above); air tank buoyancy (below)

EQUIPMENT

Cockpit and Spray Deck (Figure 11) The cockpit, seat sides and spray deck should be considered as a unit, and must of course be comfortable. The only way to find out if the cockpit will suit you is to use one for a few months, which is not much help to you when buying your first canoe. So you must at least sit inside the cockpit and think – could I sit here for up to five hours at a time? Some paddlers recently have sat there for thirty or more hours.

When you are sitting in the cockpit, check whether the seat sides hold you firmly in the canoe so that, in rough water, you can feel at one with your boat, and can sense the movement of the water. If the seat sides are too tight, you will have sore patches over your hip bones; if they're too loose, the canoe will feel 'woolly'. Press your knees up against the foredeck. Is the pressure on your knee-caps (painful) or on your thighs (comfortable). The seat sides also take the weight that is imposed upon the seat pan when you sit there. If the seat is free to sway, then bending stresses as well as straight tension will soon

26

wreck its sides. A good builder will put braces in behind the seat side (between the seat side outside and the hull inside), in order to stop seat sway. These braces can fracture in use, but if they are there, fractured or not, they will limit seat sway and repair is not difficult. A central seat brace directly under the seat is better than no brace at all, but it will not last as long as twin braces at the sides.

The spray deck fits over and tucks under the cockpit rim, where a minimum clearance of 12 mm is required. The rim edge should be sanded smooth; a sharp edge will slice the spray deck. The spray deck acts as a seal – between you and the deck edge – and prevents water flowing into the cockpit. When you get out of the cockpit, you have to use the quick-release strap, which breaks the spray deck seal.

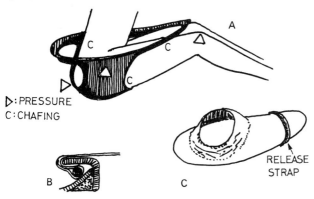

▷:PRESSURE
C:CHAFING

RELEASE STRAP

Figure 11. A cockpit; B cockpit rim with spray deck tucked under; C spray deck

Paddles Paddles – which are comprised of two blades fixed either end of a shaft – can be made in various ways. Some are simple alloy shafts with plastic sheathing to protect your hands from heat transfer via the metal shaft and blades (flat, curved or spooned) which are either plywood stiffened with hardwood ribs, or moulded plastic. More expensive paddles are made with glass

27

fibre tubular shafts and wooden blades, or shafts of wood and blades of grp. Even better are the laminated wooden paddles, where shaft and blade are made up from as many as thirty pieces of selected wood. I use jointed shafts only as spare paddles carried on the rear deck of a sea-going boat – under any kind of effort, the shaft tends to separate just when it is most needed.

If a paddle has curved or spooned blades, it will be handed. A right-handed person will normally use a right-handed paddle. To find out whether you need to use a right- or left-handed paddle, paddle around for a while using a flat bladed paddle. Ask someone to watch you – if the left blade flicks just before entering the water, then you are paddling right-handed, and vice versa. The 'flicking' of the blade is known as feathering.

To identify a handed paddle, stand a paddle on end in front of you. Turn the hollow of the lower blade towards your feet – the hollow of the upper blade is then pointing towards whichever hand it is, since the blades are set at right-angles to each other.

To find out what length of paddle suits you, stand a paddle on end beside you (Figure 12). With your feet flat on the floor, reach up so that your hand rests easily on top of the upper edge of the top blade – this is about the right length for general purposes. A white water paddler uses a slightly shorter paddle; a racing paddler a longer one; a polo player uses a very short paddle. A single blade paddle should reach from the floor to the end of your chin or nose.

To establish your grasp, place the centre of the shaft horizontally on top of your head. Your hands should hold the shaft so that both elbows make a right angle (Figure 13A). Lower the paddle in front of you and see where your hands are placed for the normal hold. A white water paddler takes a narrower grasp, a racing paddler a wider grasp, and a polo player can only just get his hands on the shaft, so close together are the blades. A single blade paddle should be held in both hands, a little more than shoulder width apart, with one hand on top of

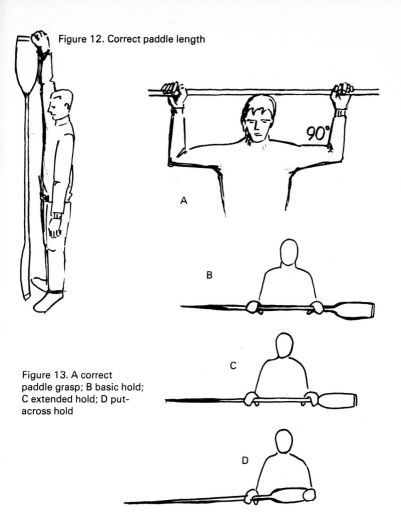

Figure 12. Correct paddle length

Figure 13. A correct
paddle grasp; B basic hold;
C extended hold; D put-
across hold

the paddle, with the paddle carried horizontally across
your chest.

Three basic holds are possible with the double blade:
normal – as described above (13B); extended – with your
hands normal distance apart, but with one hand
touching the blade on that side (13C); or put-across –
where your hands are about shoulder width apart, but
one hand holds the outer end of the blade (13D).

29

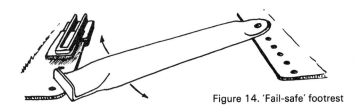

Figure 14. 'Fail-safe' footrest

Footrest To avoid the possibility of being trapped inside your canoe, you must use a fail-safe footrest.* A footrest which is fixed at both ends to the inside of the hull can fail and, in so doing, your feet will become trapped, since the bar acts as a latch which holds your feet down inside the hull. You are then not able to use your paddle, or to recover from a capsize. The fail-safe system is shown in Figure 14. One end of the footrest is pivoted, the other end is held in a clip, so that if your feet do go past the bar, it is possible to pull them free, as the bar can open away from the clip.

Deck Rigging Deck lines are necessary for use in deep water rescues, when towing, and for grasping in difficulties in capsizes. They are also used to stow equipment on deck. There are various ways of rigging a deck, and you will have to decide which is the best method for you. Figure 15 shows the method I use, but you should bear the following points in mind:

1   End toggles (15A), attached to the canoe by a single line, are useful when carrying a canoe, or when capturing a loose canoe.
2   End loops can trap your fingers, and can actually twist off the end finger joint of a swimmer who holds on when rolling over and over in waves or in rivers.
3   You can tow a canoe from either a central point on deck just behind the cockpit, or from the rear end. The former method is better for the directional

*The Tie-Beam Fail-Safe Footrest is patented and is available from Valley Canoe Products, Private Road, 4 Colwick Estate, Nottingham.

control of the towing boat; the latter method tends to cause the towing canoe to point away from the towed canoe.

4 Loose deck lines alongside the cockpit can trap you when you are rolling since, as you roll, the line is wrapped around the hull.

5 Floating deck lines (15B) are useful for grabbing in a capsize. 5 or 6 mm nylon line that stretches is best; 3 strand laid line can be spliced easily.

6 Any metal or plastic device on deck, which uses a hinge of some sort, will corrode or jam solid with sand and grit. Snap shackles are usually a source of trouble. It is better to use a simple knot, the half hitch.

7 A paddle park (15D) in front of the cockpit is very useful for paddles and loose gear. A rear equipment park is usually only found on sea-going kayaks.

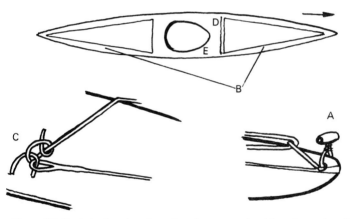

Figure 15. Deck rigging. A end toggles, the two cords whipped together; B fore and aft deck lines; C anchorage points for deck lines fore and aft each side of cockpit; D elastic paddle park (5 mm shock cord) across foredeck loops; E no line alongside cockpit

Rudder A rudder on a canoe, kayak or ski is either necessary or essential, indicated – or forbidden – by competition rules. It is always a weak spot however. For

31

maximum efficiency it should be under the rear part of the hull, where it pivots on a shaft which penetrates the bottom, and is thus a source of potential leaks. Being a fixed protrusion, it will also suffer damage if knocked against an obstacle.

The stern-hung rudder is fixed outside the hull, so no perforations are necessary, but the blade is less efficient. This rudder is also subject to accidental damage – or even deliberate damage, when a competitor may try to nobble the opposition at the start of a race.

The rudder is usually operated by foot. Several systems are used, the best being the kick-stick system (Figure 16). The kick stick is a bar which runs lengthways in the centre of the boat between your feet. You steer the rudder by knocking the stick across from one side to the other with your toes. The stick is pivoted and the rudder wires are taken back to the rudder stock. Ideally, the kick stick should end in a half circle pulley, and the rudder stock should be a circular pulley.

With the tiller bar system, your feet press against a movable bar, to the ends of which are attached the rudder wires. However, random rudder movements are common, as the movement of your feet in the paddling action tends to introduce a regular swerving motion, which the rudder is put there to prevent.

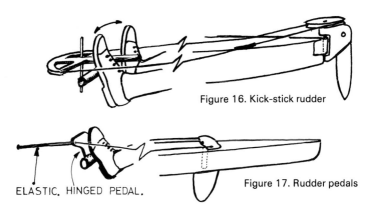

Figure 16. Kick-stick rudder

ELASTIC. HINGED PEDAL.

Figure 17. Rudder pedals

Surf skis seem to do better with rudder pedals (Figure 17). Both rudder wires have a separate pedal attached to them; each pedal moving independently from the other. You steer the pedals by pressing forwards with your toes. The action is similar to that used with a tiller bar, but if the pedals are properly adjusted, the paddling action should not affect the rudder. The rudder stock can be a simple bar, rather than a pulley, as the system is self-balancing. A refinement of this system is to add elastics to keep the pedals pulled forwards against the tension of the rudder wires. This keeps the pedals up out of the way of your feet, and the pedals can then be made self centering.

Skeg A skeg is a fixed rudder blade, usually home made by enthusiasts, which is used to 'stiffen' the canoe, ie reduce the turning ability of the hull. A well balanced kayak should not turn in a wind, but many do. Whilst the skeg takes away the strain of keeping the boat balanced on course against a cross wind, on a long trip it does add extra drag, which is felt after several hours of paddling.

DAY KIT

The minimum amount of kit which you will need for a day's canoeing is roughly as follows.

For a day trip on a river, you will need three waterproof bags.

Bag 1   Dry clothes for wearing after your trip. This is the bag in which you carried your canoeing clothing to the waterside. A separate smaller wrapper for your dirty shoes is a good idea. This bag, and the wrapper, goes in the canoe first, at the back.

Bag 2   Food – sandwiches, large bar of chocolate, apple, two cans of pop – beer if you prefer, chocolate biscuits, piece of cheese. This bag goes in the cockpit area, just behind the seat side. You may prefer to carry an extra bar of chocolate in your anorak pocket or in a pouch, for easy access.

Bag 3   Repair kit – the very basic essentials are plumber's putty tape wrapped in a polythene wrapper, and a sharp knife.

First Aid kit – a long strip of Elastoplast type dressing; a small pair of scissors; a tube of ointment; wasp sting spray; triangular bandage; matches in a waterproof can – say a film can with a small piece of sandpaper inside the lid. This bag goes in just behind the cockpit.

For a day trip at sea, you will need a waterproof bag and two wide-necked plastic jars, 4.5 litre size.

Bag   The clothing is dealt with as above. You should also include a spare anorak and a pair of windproof over-trousers. You could survive wearing nothing else if necessary.

Jar 1   Repair kit – for you and the canoe. This should include a waterproof torch, with good batteries. Matches to light a fire – there is plenty of wood on some remote beaches. Two flares, one being a parachute flare such as the Icarus: it's expensive, but it does attract attention. The other flare might be a hand held model. Beware of buying cardboard cased flares, as it is quite impossible to keep these dry. It is a good idea to have the flare attached to your person, say in a pouch on your lifejacket.

Jar 2   Food and drink sufficient for the day and a night. A flask of hot soup or a hot drink is very welcome. You should also include in this jar a large plastic bag – about 1 x 2 m, made of orange coloured polythene sheet. A bivouac is possible in such a bag. You will still be wet, but not too cold. A small towel, long enough to wrap around your neck like a scarf is useful – and a woollen hat.

These two jars are fixed under elastics on the rear deck, and are tethered there as well. In an emergency you can grab the gear and go – say if you are stranded on a beach, and have to survive overnight. On the fore deck you might have a deck chart, and a simple compass. There are many ways of preparing for sea trips, and I advise you to read other specialist books on the subject (see the book list on page 94).

More advanced paddlers will know what they will need for longer trips.

REPAIRS

There are two types of repair – the short term emergency repair, either in camp or on the water, and the long term workshop repair. Long term workshop repairs require the use of grp materials, and I would suggest you consult my other books on this subject (see book list).

Repairs to your canoe can be made on the water in calm conditions, when your boat can be lifted temporarily out of the water by using the rafting method (see page 44). I usually use patches cut from a roll of 5 cm-wide plumber's tape whilst slalom enthusiasts prefer to use 5 cm-wide electrician's tape, which is rather expensive; or a thin, brown packing tape which stretches onto the damaged part of the hull. The plumber's tape and the electrician's tape will stick to a wet hull, but the packing tape has to be used on a dry hull.

You can also use a piece of foam plastic sponge, about the size of a small loaf of bread. In an emergency, you can push this into a hole or crack in a grp canoe from the inside. There is a bulge of plastic on the outside of the hull, but the sponge helps to resist abrasive damage, and it can easily be pushed back into place if dislodged. A slow seepage of water persists, but the use of a sponge gives a longer time between bailing out sessions.

5 Elementary Work

CARRYING YOUR CANOE

Lay your canoe on the ground, facing the way you want to go. Kneel beside it on the left, and reach into the cockpit with your right hand, fingers under the rim, thumb upwards. Grasp the right hand side of the rim with your right hand, and use your left hand to pull the canoe on to your thighs. Now, roll the canoe up onto your right shoulder. Stand up, and hoist the canoe high on to your shoulder. Tuck your right elbow close to your chest, with your hand pressing up to take some of the weight off your shoulder – you should take some of it on your hip. Walk across to your paddle, and put your left toe under the exact centre of the shaft. Flick up with your toe, and grasp the shaft in your left hand. Off you go.

LAUNCHING YOUR CANOE

When you reach the waterside, drop the paddle on the ground and then slide the canoe off your shoulder, stern first. Grasp the cockpit rim and lower the canoe across your thighs. (In Figure 19 the paddle is already in the cockpit. Don't do this – you could lose all if the canoe drifts away. If your paddle is on the bank or shore, you at least have a 2 m extension to your reach if your canoe drifts away.) On a river, your canoe should now be alongside the bank, facing upstream, so that you can see what is happening once you have entered the cockpit, and the current takes charge. On a beach, lower your

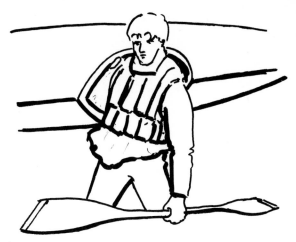

Figure 18. Carrying your canoe

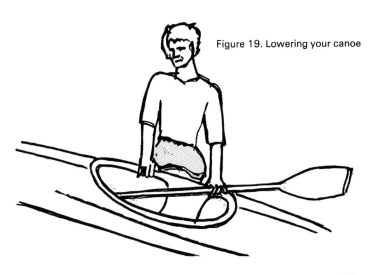

Figure 19. Lowering your canoe

canoe to the sand about 3 m from the water, then drag it forwards by the toggle until it's in water about 5-10 cm deep.

ENTERING THE COCKPIT

There are two ways to go afloat in a canoe. You can either launch the canoe and then get in; or you can get in first, and then launch the canoe.

Entering a Floating Canoe Sit on the bank on the left side of your canoe, facing the bow. Put your feet onto the floor in front of the seat, and place your right hand on the *centre* rear of the cockpit rim, with your fingers inside the rim. Now swing your body weight off your behind into the seat, taking your weight on both arms. Straighten your legs and sit down. (This is when you will find that your footrest requires adjustment.)

Another useful method, which is more adaptable, is as follows (Figure 20). Sit on the bank on the left side of your canoe, and lay your paddle across the rear of the cockpit, with the blade flat on the bank. Place your right hand on the *centre* rear of the cockpit. Your fingers should be inside the rim, with your thumb over the shaft of the paddle, the shaft lying just behind the rim. Sit on the shaft, but only on the bank side where it touches the rear deck. If you sit on its middle, you will smash the shaft. Place your feet in the canoe, and slide your legs down into position – then slide off the shaft into the seat.

Whatever method you use, it is always a good idea to hitch up the spray deck across your buttocks, so that the spray deck isn't trapped under you when you sit down.

Now, are you comfortable? If you are touring, can you stretch out your legs. If you are going into rough water, are your legs jammed tight up under the deck or thigh braces? Adjust the footrest bar until it feels right.

Next you must fix the spray deck onto the cockpit rim, as follows. First, ensure that the release strap is properly secured, and that it is outside the deck, then reach

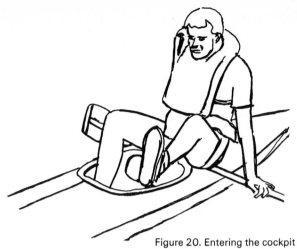

Figure 20. Entering the cockpit

behind you and pull the elastic edge of the spray deck across and under the rear of the cockpit rim. Using both hands together, ease the elasticated edge of the spray deck forwards and under the cockpit rim until it's in front of your hips. Again check that the release strap is outside the spray deck, and pull the front of the spray deck over the cockpit rim. Ease the sides of the spray deck over the cockpit rim. Check that the end of your life-jacket strap has not been trapped between the rim and the spray deck. Ease the strap out, or your body movement will pull off the spray deck. Check that the spray deck release strap works, by pulling it outwards and upwards. Refix.

Be careful – if the spray deck elastic is exposed because the stitching has failed, then the exposed part will not pull off the cockpit rim as it should. You could be trapped, hooked on to your canoe by the elastic. A stitch in time – saves one of your nine lives.

Seal Launch This is used when you have to launch your canoe sideways off rocks etc, or endways off muddy shores, pebbly beaches etc. You will of course enter the cockpit on land, and adjust your spray deck and footrest.

A sideways launch should not be used for a drop down to the water of more than a metre or so, or you will smash the seat attachments as you hit the water. The action is to brace yourself tightly into the cockpit, and lean well out to the side as for a draw stroke (see page 50). When the canoe starts to slip, draw hard outwards to the water and you will slide off the rocks. An endways launch is especially useful off muddy banks or to go into a deep pool, say 2 m of water. Bows first, you have to shove off energetically from the bank. Don't be half hearted though, or the end will not slide off the bank easily, and the canoe may turn over.

BALANCE

Once you are afloat, take the paddle in both hands and check that your grasp is correct. Then, raise the paddle high above your head, in what I call the Geronimo position. Now rock the canoe from side to side using your hips (Figure 21). You will be pleasantly surprised just how much tilt can be obtained without falling in. Remember though, that in going out through surf, or when you hit a roaring wall of water on a river, the

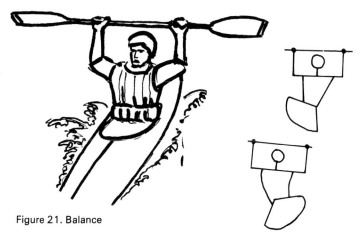

Figure 21. Balance

natural tendency is to hold the paddle high above your head. This course of action lines up your unprotected face for a swift thump with a great weight of water, and you cannot then paddle through to comparative safety on the other side. If you are in difficulty, put the paddle blade *in the water* and use it energetically (see page 88).

HAND PADDLING

Now put your paddle down out of the way. Please have someone ready to throw your paddle to you though, or to pull you out if you need help. Use your hands to move about. Practice the following – using your hands any way you can.

Go forwards.　　Go backwards.　Turn to your left and your right.　　Move sideways to left and to right.　　Capsize.

CAPSIZE

Your first capsize. You'll be upside down with time to think about it. Water will be going up your nose and making it hurt. It will be cold in the water possibly. It will be dark too. You will be looking, or rather feeling, for the spray deck release strap. There is no need to worry, if you follow the following procedure. But don't forget to have a helper available, to perform a swimmer-canoeist rescue (see page 67) if necessary.

For your first few capsizes only, remove your spray deck. Then, place your hands under the canoe about level with your feet – this is known as the 'laid forward' position. Leaning backwards tends to lock you into the cockpit, which can cause problems. With your hands clasped around the outside of the canoe, take a deep breath, and rock over. Keep your head down. As you go under the water, start breathing out gently through your nose – this keeps the water out of it. Now put your hands each side of the cockpit, about level with your hips. With your body still curled up forwards, push the canoe off your legs, letting them go limp and straight. If you bend your knees you can lock yourself in the cockpit. Breathe out through your nose. Keep hold of the cockpit rim with one hand, and roll out of the cockpit and come up alongside. It is most important to keep hold of the canoe. Don't develop the bad habit of letting it drift away from you: you might be in real difficulty one day in open water, if the wind blows your canoe away and you're unable to get back in touch. Now go hand over hand to one end of the canoe. Keep the canoe upside down and then, using backstroke and holding the canoe lightly at one end, swim with the current to the bank and empty the water out of the canoe.

How was your capsize? Not good? Do it again. Good? Do it again. This time practice capsizing with your spray deck in place, and remember to pull the release strap when you are upside down. If you pull the spray deck off as you go over, you are cheating *yourself*.

EMPTYING YOUR CANOE

In shallow water stand at one end of the canoe, preferably the bows. Keeping the canoe upside down, raise the bows in the air. Now turn the canoe right way up, cockpit uppermost, still keeping the bows in the air. Now lower the bows, and press them down under the water – the water inside the canoe will run to the lower end, the

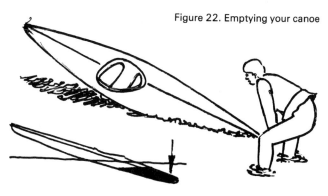

Figure 22. Emptying your canoe

bows (Figure 22). Place your hands as far along the canoe as seems comfortable, about 30 cm, one hand on top of the bows, one hand underneath. (I prefer right hand on top, left hand on the left and holding the underside of the canoe.) Without raising the bows, turn the canoe over by a quick wristy action. The cockpit is now upside down. Raise the bows at once, before more water flows into the downturned cockpit. Most of the water will now fall out of the cockpit hole. Repeat this action three or four times, which should empty the canoe. When you are used to this action, it is very quick and you can empty a canoe in twenty seconds.

If the canoe is very full of water, it will first be necessary to lift the canoe up and spill as much water out of the cockpit as possible.

Stand alongside your canoe. It is easier to empty if you are in chest deep water, so that you can get your shoulder under the cockpit rim. If you are in shallow water, raise the canoe, cockpit inwards, against your legs. Provided that the lower edge of the cockpit rim is under water, and the upper edge is above water, and you apply a steady lifting force, the water will flow out of the cockpit and air will flow in. There will come a point when you can no longer execute this action easily – you must then progress to the method of emptying just described.

A surf ski never requires this treatment.

COMING ALONGSIDE

Casting off from the bank is easy enough to do, but coming alongside at a given point requires some practice. Imagine that you are on a slow moving stream. A friend is standing on the bank, say on a jetty or landing stage, and you want to come alongside him (Figure 23). (Assume that the current is flowing from left to right of the page.)

From a distance of about 9 m – two canoe lengths – paddle directly, at quarter speed, towards your friend on the bank. The current will move you away downstream

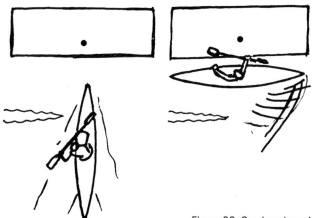

Figure 23. Coming alongside

slightly. When the bows are about 60 cm from the bank, put your upstream (left) paddle blade in the water and hold it steady there as a brake. The canoe will then start to turn. If you start to turn too far out, you will overdo it and come in stern first; if you leave it too late, you might ram the bank.

If you use a slalom type of canoe it will turn very easily, and as it starts to skid sideways it will put you alongside very smoothly. If you use a directionally stable canoe, ie one that is slow to turn, you must either start to turn earlier, or further out from the bank. In the latter case I would prefer to approach the position from downstream, up against the current. Come up to the mark slowly, so as not to overshoot.

RAFTING

A development of coming alongside, if you are in a group, is to form a raft of canoes – eight is the maximum manageable number. One person starts the raft, ie just sits there waiting to be joined. Each canoe then comes alongside as you would for a jetty, or in from behind going forwards or in from in front going backwards. It isn't easy at first, especially as it may be the first time you have had to try and put the canoe anywhere precisely. To break up the raft, canoes leave alternately forwards and backwards, thus affording each canoeist the maximum possible amount of water when moving away from the tightly packed bunch in a raft (Figure 24). Swift exit may be necessary above a weir, or as a rowing eight comes belting down the river. This technique is also useful on open water to share out food and drink, and to have a rest.

Whilst in the raft, you hold the cockpit rim of the canoe alongside you. The end paddlers hold their paddles only – they are attached to the raft by the next canoeist. It is possible, if you are sufficiently skilled, to hold your paddle as in Figure 25, and to grasp the next cockpit with your other hand. The end paddles can be used to manoeuvre the whole raft. If both end paddlers paddle forwards, the raft moves forwards, and vice versa. If one paddles forwards, the other backwards, the raft turns quite easily. This is a good way to learn how the basic strokes affect the canoe. You can then break up the raft, and reform with different paddlers at the ends.

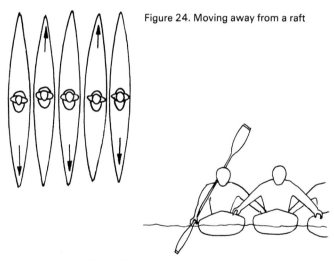

Figure 24. Moving away from a raft

Figure 25. End paddler paddle grip

45

6 Basic Strokes

PADDLE USE

The paddle can be used either as a lever, moved about by the paddler – dynamic actions; or it can be used as a deflector, when the water movement around the canoe and the paddle blade provides the required energy – static actions.

The dynamic actions are described in this chapter, and the static actions in chapter 7.

PADDLING FORWARDS

The most efficient action is the racing stroke. It will take a great deal of practice, and informed criticism, to achieve an effective, natural action, but it is important to develop a good style – it's rather like developing a good golf swing. The basic action is as follows:

Lean forward in the cockpit. Your left leg should be bent, your left hand just in front of your left knee, your right hand about eye level. Keep your fingers relaxed. Now, put the left blade into the water (Figure 26), and straighten your left leg. As your left hand comes back to hip level, thrust your head further forward and straighten your right arm (Figure 27). In Figure 28 you are between strokes. Note that your head is well forward, your shoulders turned into line with the boat – this position lengthens the stride of your stroke, useful for when you are performing a sprint start. The paddle is held like a lance at shoulder level. Your left leg is bent, ready to kick straight as the left blade enters the water.

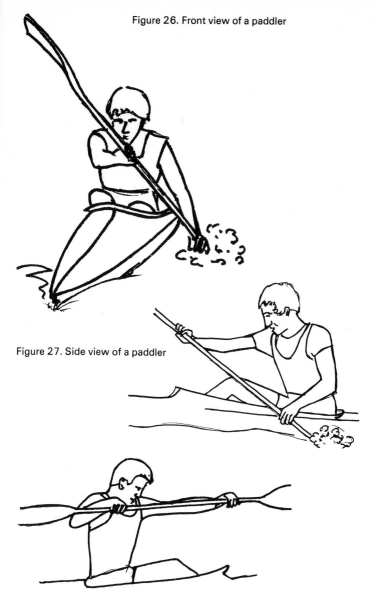

Figure 26. Front view of a paddler

Figure 27. Side view of a paddler

Figure 28. Side view of another paddler, sprint start

47

Try and remember the following points when you are paddling, and especially when you are tired.

1 Sit up; sit forward.
2 Use your shoulders.
3 Keep the blade close to the boat.
4 Reach well forward; lift the blade out early.

STOPPING AND PADDLING BACKWARDS

You can stop in several ways. You can ram the bank – provided it is soft – or run up a beach. You can turn the hull sideways, which puts the brakes on very quickly. However, the basic way is simply to paddle backwards, as follows.

Put the paddle blade, shaft upright, in the water behind you, about where you pull it out on the forward action. Bear down upon the paddle, pushing it forwards. Try and drive it deep into the water close to the hull. Pull back hard on your upper arm, which should be bent; your lower arm is trying to straighten forwards. Lean backwards – you should by now have stopped. You can in fact stop from any speed on flat water in four strokes.

If you want to continue paddling backwards, put the left blade in the water and hold it there for one second (literally). Repeat with the right blade. (Note that the canoe swerves violently around the braking blade; one swerve must be used to cancel the other swerve.) Now push the left blade in again, and push it forwards. Repeat with the right blade – you should by now be going backwards. Remember to look over your shoulder so that you can see where you are going.

When you are surfing, the most effective way to stop in an unbroken wave is to capsize. If the wave has broken, you won't stop until the wave has flattened out, usually very close to the beach.

SWEEP TURN

This stroke is used to turn the boat – either when it's

Figure 29. Sweep turn

stationary, or when it's moving. The stroke can be done to your right or left, forwards or backwards, and can also be developed into the low telemark, which is used in surfing and on rivers. It is a basic stroke which figures in the proficiency certificate tests of the British Canoe Union. For the reverse right sweep turn, practice the following (Figure 29).

Sit up straight, and hold the paddle in the normal grasp. Put the right blade, edge vertical, into the water at the right rear of the hull. The blade should be touching the hull. Now, look at the blade, and keep looking at it. Your right arm is almost straight, extended backwards; your left arm, hand held low, is taken right across your chest. Keeping your right arm straight all the way, sweep the blade in an arc from the back of the hull to a point at right angles to the centre line of the hull. Lift the blade out of the water, put it back into the water beside the rear of the hull, and repeat the process.

Try the left reverse sweep turn, the right forward sweep turn and the left forward sweep turn. Practice alternate sweep turns, ie forward right alternating with reverse left, and vice versa.

DIRECTION CORRECTION

The first problem that you will find when you start

paddling a kayak is that it will not go straight, ie that the bows swerve. Slalom kayaks are the least stable directionally – you can correct them whilst on the move as follows.

Say the bows are heading to the left. As the swerve develops, you will hear a bubbling of water under the stern, as it slides sideways to the right. The correction must be applied before the swerve and bubbling happen. Without breaking stroke, on the next left blade entry take the paddle round away from the hull, as in a sweep turn. The blade should be vertical, relative to the water surface. The next point is crucial. Your left arm *must* be straight as the blade is taken right round to the rear and is clapped up tight against the hull. Keep looking at the blade; doing so will help the body turn. The swerve should now have stopped. You can overdo it however, and swerve the other way. Experience will guide your efforts and soon you will hardly notice the break in your smooth paddling action, as a tiny correction is automatically applied almost unconsciously, before the swerve has time to develop.

Remember, if you swerve to the right, you must correct on the right; and vice versa.

DRAW STROKE

This is an essential stroke for any vigorous rough water work, where the ability to move the canoe sideways in a moment, as a reflex action done without conscious thought, is the best guarantee of safety in rock-studded fast-moving water. The basic stroke is as follows.

Hold your paddle in the normal grip, with your thumbs turned inwards. Keep the paddle shaft vertical, and put one blade into the water, about opposite the middle of your thigh. The flat side of the blade should touch the hull (Figure 30). Now, turn the blade at right angles, and slide it sideways away from the hull, keeping it in line with your mid-thigh. When the blade is about 60 cm away from the hull, and the shaft is now tilted, again turn the blade flat side towards the hull, still on the imaginary line. Your upper hand must be far across your body. Now pull with your lower hand – the blade will move in towards the hull, whilst the hull moves out towards the blade. Provided that the action is directly towards the centre of gravity (approximately mid-thigh), and the blade is exactly at right angles to the line of travel of the paddle, then the canoe will move sideways without turning. If the canoe does turn, your action is not yet correct. Learn to get it right now, as follows. When the blade is about 8-10 cm from the hull side, turn the blade so that it is slicing through the water, and repeat the whole movement. As you gain in confidence, start to lean on to the paddle as it moves in towards the boat. This action improves the paddle's 'bite' in the water, and extra power is given to the movement.

Note especially that as your lower hand is pulling in towards the boat, your upper hand is moving further across your body, pushing in the direction that the canoe is required to move, just as in the forward paddling stroke. There is often a tendency to pull back with your upper hand, more or less parallel to the movement of

Figure 30. Draw stroke

your lower hand. This takes all the power out of the action, and must be avoided.

Now practice the following variations. Their purpose is to improve surfing in a broached position, so that the correction of spin on a surfing wave is made possible.

1 Start the drawstroke action well forwards of the cockpit, and keep the paddle blade moving on a line drawn through mid-calf, at right angles to the canoe. This will cause the canoe to turn with its bows leading, as well as to move sideways.

2 Start the action as far behind the cockpit as you can reach. As the action develops, the canoe will move sideways, stern leading.

3 Start the action well forwards and out to one side. Move the blade on a diagonal line, originating from mid-thigh. The canoe will then move forwards, and to one side, without turning. Try the same action towards the rear.

SUPPORT STROKE

This stroke is similar to an advanced draw stroke. In fact, most advanced white water canoeists do not use the formal support stroke, but simply turn the paddling action into a support on a vertical shaft. However, it is better to learn the simple support stroke, and then find out how it and the draw stroke merge into one all purpose correction stroke.

Hold the paddle in the normal grasp. With your outer arm almost straight, reach out to one side with the paddle; the blade must be flat on the water. Now raise the blade about 30 cm above the water, and slap the blade straight down onto the water surface. You will feel a kick over to the opposite side as the blade hits the water. To correct this kick away from the blade, lean towards the side where the blade is to slap before you slap the blade down. The kick back will then lift you upright again. However, as you fall further over, and more power is generated, the paddle could be broken with the slap. So, stop the slap at an early stage, and fall over towards the blade which is already flat *on* the water, and not *above* it. Regain the upright position by thrusting down on the blade.

Novices are often slow with this action, and the blade sinks down through the water. To bring the blade up to the surface again quickly, turn it at right angles and slice it back up to the surface. As you gain confidence, and the feeling of support is developed, try leaning further and further over, until the point of balance is passed, and the canoe will turn over unless the stroke is successful. Hip flick movement is useful here (see page 61). Remember to keep your head low during this stroke.

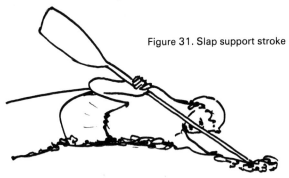

Figure 31. Slap support stroke

Now that you've developed confidence, try the following. Perform an off-balance support stroke on one side, then immediately sit up and fall over onto the other side, and perform an opposite side support. Sit up and repeat. You will find that your action becomes an easy swinging movement. Your outer arm on each stroke should be deep in the water, so that your shoulders go under and the water just touches your ear (Figure 31). The action has a rhythm which must be learned, and practising this goes hand in hand with learning to roll.

Now try a series of opposite side draw strokes, leaning further and further onto the blade, so that the canoe leaps from side to side. You will find that the support stroke on a vertical paddle is just the same as a draw stroke when taken to the extreme position.

Sculling support stroke, using extended grip

Tim Swale, at Cenarth Falls, about to perform a left forward sweep turn.
Note his paddle shaft is low, with the blade a bit wide from the kayak
side and about to enter the water

7 Advanced Strokes

To turn on the spot in a stationary canoe requires a dynamic stroke, the sweep turn. To turn whilst moving quickly through the water requires a static stroke, with the blade acting as a rudder. The basic static strokes are the stern rudder and the bow rudder.

STERN RUDDER

This is used to turn the canoe to the left or right whilst you are slowing down. It is used on surf when turning the kayak from side to side, and to hold the kayak back on the face of a wave, in order not to run out in front of it. It is useful for coming alongside a river bank or jetty, or into a raft of canoes. The left stern rudder, for example, is performed as follows.

Sit up straight, and hold the paddle in the normal grasp. Put the paddle shaft along the left of the hull, the left blade, edge vertical, should nearly touch the stern. Your left arm should be straight, with your shoulders turned almost into line with the boat. Now move forwards and then drop the blade into the water. The boat should turn gently to the left. Try this action to your right with your arm straight; and on the left and right with your arm bent.

BOW RUDDER

Sit up straight, and hold the paddle in the normal grasp. For a right bow rudder, put the right blade, edge vertical, into the water on the right side of the bow. The paddle shaft is taken right across your body, with the left blade laid over your right shoulder (Figure 32). Take position, paddling gently forwards. The canoe should turn towards the paddle blade. Hold the paddle tightly, as it tends to want to pull out of your grasp, especially as you go faster. If the blade then wrenches at your hand, either let it go – which is a complete confession of failure but may prevent a capsize – or, a better course of action, turn the upper edge of the blade inwards towards the canoe. This action eases the strain at once. Alternatively, you may wish to increase the speed at which you turn, in which case, you should turn the upper edge of the blade outwards.

LOW TELEMARK

The low telemark – a term borrowed from skiing – is used for turning a kayak quickly, for breaking in and breaking out on a river (see page 75), and for zigzagging when surfing, ie running along the face of a wave. It is ideal for coming alongside a river bank or jetty – the low telemark turns the boat, puts it alongside in a stylish slide, and slows it down as well.

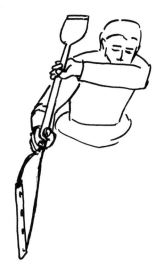

Figure 32. Bow rudder

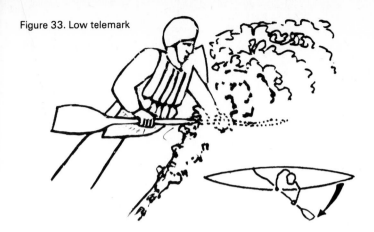

Figure 33. Low telemark

The stroke is a balancing and steering action. The paddle blade is held out to one side, where it drags at the water, and this 'drag' starts the turn. A boat with a shorter waterline, ie a slalom type of kayak, is easier to turn than one with a longer waterline. You must learn to handle different types of boat.

Before practicing the low telemark, first practice the reverse sweep turn – to right and to left. Make sure your turns are effective. Remember to keep the blade straight up and down. Now, sit up straight and on your next stroke, put the blade into the water at the rear of the hull. Your rear arm should be almost straight; your forward arm should be bent across your body, with your forward hand over the edge of the canoe on the same side as the paddle. Both hands should be held low. Now tilt the upper edge of the paddle blade forwards, and start to sweep the blade forwards through the water. Because of the tilt of the blade, it will try to ride up and stay on the surface. As you feel the lifting action of the blade, try to lean over towards the paddle as it moves forwards. You should get some support from the paddle as it moves; if it stops moving, the support ceases. Now start to move forwards slowly and try again, with your body leaning over slightly. You should start to turn quite easily towards the side on which the paddle is working.

When you feel confident with this action, go faster, lean further, try harder. The action now becomes a good capsize drill, that is, until you learn to balance your weight on the upward lift of the blade. By now, your shoulder should be close to the water surface; your lower hand should be right under the water, your upper hand just clearing the foredeck. You should try to turn the boat through 180° at one application of the blade. Try the stroke to your left and to your right.

The low telemark tends to throw the back end of most kayaks outwards, rather like a skidding car. If you are going towards an obstruction, and want to turn away from it, don't use the low telemark. The centre of gravity of the boat actually moves closer to the obstruction, even though the bows are clearing it away to one side. It is possible to come broadside onto a rock in a river. You would do better to use a high telemark (another term borrowed from skiing).

HIGH TELEMARK

The high telemark differs from the low telemark as the bow rudder differs from the stern rudder. Effectively, the high telemark is a bow rudder taken well out to one side, and enhanced by extreme body lean onto the blade in the water. The turn is used in surfing to pull off a wave which is about to break, and to haul the canoe over the crest of a wave from the broached position. It is used in a fast and rocky river to break out from behind a rock, or in slalom to flick a boat around into a gate. It is probably the most powerful of the single simple strokes. (A complicated stroke could contain, for example, as many as five different strokes – all of which take place in two seconds!)

To practice the high telemark, take up the bow rudder position, say right bow, and reach out with the blade as far from the boat as possible, which means that you will be leaning towards the paddle, and tending to capsize (Figure 34). Don't capsize, it wastes time; instead, turn

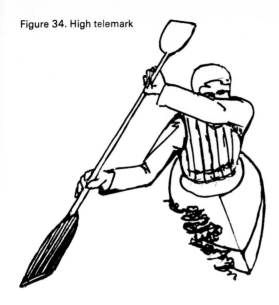

Figure 34. High telemark

the leading edge of the paddle blade outwards. Once you're in position, get up some speed, fast. Now, drop the blade into the water, well out from the side. As you feel the water pressure on the blade, lean right onto it. You may fall in, but if you get it right, the pressure of water against the blade will give you enough support to lie on it. Some of your weight is thereby transferred onto it; and the hull, relieved of your weight, will spin around the blade. As you gain confidence, you can improve the turn by bringing the blade onto a line about at right angles to your centre of gravity.

SCULLING

The paddle blade can be sculled through the water to produce sideways movement, diagonal and turning movement, and support. It is useful when going alongside, and a knowledge of what happens to a sculling blade is helpful when you are learning to roll.

Shaft Swing Hold the paddle in the normal grasp: *do not* reverse grasp. Place the right blade (say) in the water close alongside the canoe. Keep the paddle shaft vertical. With your right hand just above the water, and your left thumb just touching your right shoulder, swing the right blade forwards through the water (slicing), keeping the blade face to the hull. Stop the swing when your right hand is level with your knees, and slice backwards. Imagine that the paddle shaft is pivoting about a fixed point between your hands, and repeat the action until the blade is moving through a 1 m swing, parallel to the canoe.

Blade Angle Keeping the swing going as above, angle the leading edge of the blade away from the canoe. Note that the leading edge changes on each swing of the shaft, ie the front edge is the leading edge on the forward scull, and vice versa, which means that the blade angle must be changed on each swing. The angle of attack must be the same on both the forward and the reverse swing, or else the canoe will turn. The angle of attack (optimum 30°) is the angle between the line of swing of the blade, and the line drawn from edge to edge of the blade. Remember that the same face of the blade must always face the canoe.

Further Developments

1 Alter the angle of attack of the leading edge from facing away from the canoe to facing in towards the canoe. This action deflects water away from the canoe, and pushes the canoe away from the paddle side.
2 Alter the angle of attack on each swing to produce a controlled turn-cum-draw stroke.
3 Change the line of swing from parallel to the canoe to an angle to the canoe, and try to achieve a controlled diagonal movement.

ROLLING

There are four basic ways to roll – down left up right; down right up left; leaning forwards (laid forward); leaning backwards (laid back) – each with its variations. The power for each roll comes, not from your arms, but from the action of your body. This power is developed in two ways: by a jack-knife action, when you are laid forward at the end of the roll; by a body twist – when you are laid back at the end of the roll. The power so developed is released, almost explosively, with the hip flick (see below).

Rolling is an essential skill in surfing, and on rough rivers, and is a method of self rescue. Rolling can also be used by rescuers to assist an inert patient out of the water onto a roller's deck. Some instructors teach rolling as the first skill, so that a novice, when learning other new strokes, can roll up out of the water if he makes any mistakes – and thus save time.

The first roll you learn to do well is usually the roll you fall back on when you are in difficulties – the screw roll. It's a mixed roll, starting off laid forward and ending up laid back. The hip flick drill is detailed next, and then the steps for learning the roll.

First Practice – Hip Flick

You should, of course, practice the hip flick in still water – say in a swimming pool. Any form of support will do for this drill: the bath side rail, your assistant's hands and arms or, preferably, a float – a fully inflated BSS 3595 lifejacket is the most suitable. It is a good idea to try a swimmer-canoeist rescue to start with, in order to gain confidence (see page 67). The hip flick drill is as follows:

1   Sit in the canoe; your assistant stands waist deep in the water, on your left side.
2   Check that your spray deck and release strap are properly adjusted. Your feet should be tight up against your footrest. Remember to wear a nose clip.

3   Take your float in your right hand, and extend your right arm out to your side.
4   Lean back along the rear deck, so that your head touches it. Keep your neck relaxed (Figure 35).
5   Now turn the canoe over onto the float side. Feel the canoe flip over.
6   Keeping your head down on the rear deck, and your chin on your right shoulder, use your hips to flick the canoe back on to balance. Repeat the action rapidly.
7   Reverse all the above instructions, and practice on your left side.

Figure 35. Hip flick starting position

Note to Assistant

8   Observe the roller's neck muscles. Are they tight, corded? Tell him to relax. His head must loll back along the rear deck, with his chin to the right.

By practising the above action, you will acquire gradually a well-timed hip flick, and a relaxed neck. Once you have achieved a reliable hip flick action, you can reduce the size of your float to a swimming training float, or even to a piece of plywood about the size of a table tennis bat.

Second Practice – 'Wind Up' Position

9   Take the paddle in the normal grasp.
10 Lay the paddle along the left side deck, with the right blade forwards, edge vertical.
11 Your right arm should be across your body, the elbow slightly crooked, your knuckles touching the deck.

62

Figure 36. 'Wind-up' position

12   Your left arm should be straight back from the shoulder, with your elbow well back, your knuckles touching the deck (Figure 36).

13   Turn the upper edge of your vertical right blade away from the canoe by 30°.

Note to Assistant

14   Check the roller's position. The rear blade should lie flat to the angle of the deck.

Third Practice – Wet Drill, Assisted

15   Your assistant stands on the right side of your bows. Again, remember to fit your nose clip.

16   Wind up as in the second practice, then lower your head into the crook of your right arm.

17   Your assistant should hold the bows in his right hand, and reach under the hull with his left hand to feel the lower edge of the right blade (Figure 37). This is quite difficult for your assistant to do.

18   Your assistant should stand so that he will be clear of the paddle blade when you strike.

Figure 37. Rolling – wet drill, assisted

19   When you roll over, your right blade comes into your assistant's left hand.

20   As this happens, your assistant *shoves* the bows away with his right hand.

21   Your assistant now supports your paddle blade as you start to lean back – and roll.

22   You now roll down left over the paddle shaft.

23   You are now underneath the water – pause for a couple of seconds. You will feel the boat turn suddenly. Now – strike.

24   Swing the paddle away from the boat side, and reach out across the water. Lean back.

25   Hip flick as soon as your head touches the rear deck, as in 6 above.

(NB. A good roller starts the hip flick sooner, but that is a matter of timing which must be learned.)

Note to Assistant

26   When you hurl the bows away from you, this action puts the roller's body into a good position for rolling. There should be at least 45° between the line of the canoe and the line of the paddle shaft before the strike begins (Figure 38).

27   Did the paddler relax his head against the rear deck, his chin to the right? He *must* do this.

28   If some support is needed because the attempt has failed, always support the paddler under the right armpit. Anyone may flail about a bit on failing, and the correct grasp will avoid misunderstandings.

Fourth Practice – Unassisted

29   Your assistant should be available for 'rescue', if required.

30   Check your equipment as in 2 above.

31   Take the paddle in the normal grasp, and cock your wrists up, so that your knuckles touch the deck.

32   The fore blade should be vertical, the upper edge turned outwards 30°.

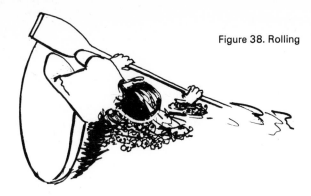

Figure 38. Rolling

33 Make sure your nose clip is adjusted, then lower your head forwards into the crook of your forward arm.
34 Two second pause upside down, remember.
35 Now turn over the paddle shaft. Pause.
36 Reach out with the paddle from the canoe side.
37 Swing out wide, and start turning upwards.
38 As your head touches the rear deck, hip flick with *power*.

Never practice failure. Let's say you fail on point 38 – go back to points 15 to 25. If you fail on point 25, go back to points 1 to 14 and build up again.

Once you have learned how to roll in sheltered or still water, practice in rough water. The easiest place is in 60 cm-high waves. Lie parallel to the wave and, as it hits you, roll over towards the shore. If you roll the other way, you won't succeed, as the wave will oppose you.

Nick Baker, American student, using Steyr roll in Atlantic College pool

Tim Swale on a Grade III rapid, Abbey Bridge on the River Tees

8 Rescue and Exposure

SWIMMER-CANOEIST RESCUE

Many rescue techniques exist, and one of the most useful is the swimmer to canoeist rescue. As you start to learn the most advanced strokes, and rolling, you will capsize. If you're using a kayak, baling out and emptying the hull is always a nuisance: however, if you stay in the cockpit and rely upon an assistant to do the 'rescue', time is saved and confidence is gained. The technique is as follows (Figure 39):

Let's say you are the 'assistant'. Swim to the upturned hull, and lie across it so that your hips are on the hull. Now lean right over, reach down into the water, and grasp the paddler's arm or hand. It is possible simply to grasp the cockpit rim, but this requires more strength. Now, lean well back, and urge the paddler upwards on the side away from you. It is possible to make this a very quick movement, and the sudden snatch could injure the

Figure 39. Swimmer-canoeist rescue

paddler's arm or shoulder. Take care also that you do not pull the paddler right up and over onto you, or you will have another rescue to perform. The paddler can help you by either lying well back, or well forward.

TWO MAN RAFT

The two man raft, on a river, is used when passing under low bridges, or when stopping on a long journey for a drink and a rest. At sea, a member of a group may become cramped and unhappy: it is quite possible for him to swap canoes, and even to lie out across the two canoe foredecks and exercise his legs. Furthermore, the raft's stability forms an essential part in any rescue operation. It can also be used when playing games, to accustom novices to using canoes. Practice this move, as follows:

Two paddlers come alongside, facing opposite ways. The 'rescuer' leans right across the foredeck of the other canoe, facing his partner – who is on his right, say. The paddles are laid across the two canoes so that the rescuer can hold them in his left hand, with which he should also grip the centre front of the other cockpit rim. The rescuer's right hand is right across the other side of the other canoe, and should be positioned as far as possible down the hull. The rescuer's chest should be pressed

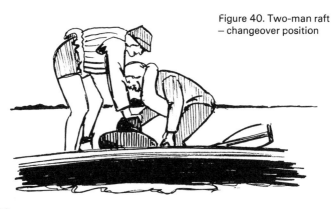

Figure 40. Two-man raft
– changeover position

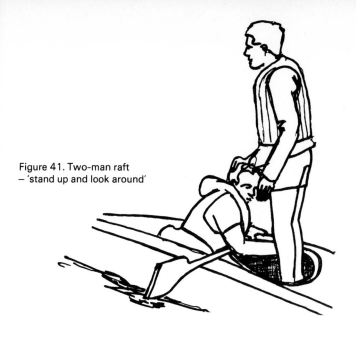

Figure 41. Two-man raft
– 'stand up and look around'

against the foredeck of the other. This last point is crucial: it adds very much to the raft's stability.

The 'patient' releases his spray deck, and jumps into the water. He then climbs back in over the left side of his canoe, reaches right across to grab the rescuer's canoe side, close to the cockpit, then pulls himself up across his own cockpit, twists round and settles onto his seat. The patient then adjusts his footrest, and fixes his spray deck back into place.

When practising this move, you will find that it's quite easy to stand up and turn around. Just use your rescuer's head as a balancing post (Figure 41).

X RESCUE

The simplest, quickest and most used of any of the rescue techniques is the X rescue, so called because one canoe is rocked out over the other, the two hulls making the shape of an 'X' on the water (Figure 42). This method should only be used if there is about 10 cm or less of water inside

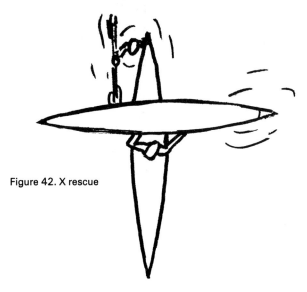

Figure 42. X rescue

the canoe. If the rescue has been slow, or if the water is rough, there may be more than 10 cm of water inside. If so, more refined drills will be required, and the 'H' rescue is the most often used, or the 'TX'.

Practice will help you acquire the necessary 'speed' and 'attack' to perform the X rescue competently, and a reasonable degree of physical strength is also required. Deck lines on the upturned canoe will certainly assist the rescuers. The details are as follows:

Go quickly to the upturned canoe. Tell the patient to relax and simply to hold on to the end of his upturned canoe, making sure that the cockpit rim stays entirely below the water. Take hold of one end of his canoe, preferably the bows. Tell the patient to hold his own paddle, your paddle, and the bows of your canoe. Make sure he is settled, or you could drift away from him. Check that your spray deck is firmly in place, or the water flowing out of his boat may flow into yours.

Now, lift the upturned bow on to your side deck (I prefer to work over the right side). Immediately haul away and pull the upturned canoe across your foredeck

Figure 43. Emptying your canoe during an X rescue

just in front of the cockpit. Don't stop until the upturned cockpit is quite clear of the water, or more water may pour in. Next, take hold of the upturned cockpit, hoist the cockpit across your cockpit, and pull it as far across your deck as you can. Try to get the cockpit right over the water on the far side. Now, lean onto the upper end of the upturned canoe. If your canoe won't tip, ask your patient to reach up and pull down the upper end (Figure 43). As soon as water stops pouring out on one tilt, reverse the tilt and drain the water out the other way. When the canoe is empty, turn the boat upright on top of your deck and then slide it into the water alongside, facing the opposite way.

You have now formed a two man raft, and your patient climbs in over the side. Some people recommend the patient's coming in from behind the two canoes. I find that this tends to force the canoes apart, and thus reduces the stability of the raft at a crucial moment. Coming in over the side, the patient's efforts pull the two canoes together, instead of spreading them apart.

Capsizes on rough water are never welcome, but are easier to deal with than capsizes on flat water, as detailed above, since the effect of the waves will do most of the work necessary to tip the water out of the boat.

EXPOSURE

Exposure is the common term for hypothermia, where the body temperature is reduced by cold, until the sufferer dies. Everyone experiences hypothermia, even on warm days, but it rarely becomes more than an attack of shivering. Remember that this is a medical problem, and I am not a medical man: but I have been to stage three of the condition, and survived to remember it. There are basically four stages, as follows:

1   Chilling of your extremities. Your hands are painful; your feet, nose, lips, ears, all hurt with cold. Shivering begins.
2   Your limb movements are slowed, and your extremities become numb. Shivering is no longer noticeable: it may stop as you become colder, and does stop in stage three. Your respiration will be shallow and rapid. Your speech is limited and may stop. Your mind becomes affected – anxiety is felt, even panic; when the latter passes, a numbness of spirit is probable – a sense of not caring very much.
3   Your limbs are almost immobile. Your speech has gone. Your hearing has dulled to the point of deafness. Your sight becomes affected – tunnel vision develops, and your colour balance is all wrong. If you're swimming, the need to time your intake of air with the surges of the waves doesn't seem to be important, and drowning may commence through carelessness.
4   You're no longer conscious, no longer moving. Your heart is only just beating. Only skilled care and a great deal of luck will revive you.

Well, what can you do? There you are on a river bank in winter, snow all around, the nearest road a mile away, and no warmth available. Or you are on a rock in a skerry system a mile off the coast. Your companion is suffering from all the symptoms in stage 3. You must, if you can, do this:

1   Stop the loss of bodily warmth. Wrap him in a windproof bag – the exposure bag.
2   Feed him a hot drink. Alcohol has unlooked for effects, so *don't use it*.
3   Stop the loss of heat to the ground by conduction –

put something under the bag, even it it's only heaps of wet seaweed. Keep his head lower than his feet.

4   If you can, strip off his clothes, and your clothes, so as to enhance the flow of warmth from one body to the other. (Clothes are designed to reduce heat transfer.) Get in the bag with him, and cuddle the body close and use your warmth to assist him. Mind you don't start to lose heat too fast yourself, or there will be two casualties.

   This is an extreme step, and will only be essential as your patient slides away into stage 4.

5   If he starts to shiver again, that's fine, because he is returning through the stages. But now is the time when drinks and food will be necessary, to sustain him through a very tiring time. Powerful shivering is *very, very* exhausting, and there is no way to stop it except by warming him up to normal body heat.

Naturally, one's first duty is to obtain medical aid. But the first aid outlined above may just help enough until skilled help does arrive. Canoeing, at its best, tends to take place in remote spots.

(left) Dave Holmes, using a BAT Mk 6 on grade 4 water, is about to vanish under a stopper at the bottom of a rapid on the Tees. Note how he is bearing down, deep onto the right blade, in order to bring the boat down the centre of the spout

(below) Tim Swale has just completed a forward loop and pop-out, by approaching the stopper from below the fall — when the mass of water slammed down on the bows, the back of the kayak reared up vertically and threw him into the loop. He is now moving backwards, digging down to his left with the paddle blade, to seek bite on it and so balance on his paddle shaft. A cautionary note: only play in stoppers like this, when the water level is normal

9 Rivers

LEARNING ABOUT RIVERS

You must always remember that rivers run across land which belongs to someone, and as such, you should ask permission to use any particular stretch of water. Don't canoe near anglers; they are enjoying their sport just as much as you are. The most sensible idea before you embark on a river trip of any kind, is to contact the British Canoe Union, which has river advisers who offer advice to paid up members of the BCU, and also publishes *Guide to Waterways*.

Figure 44 (pages 76-77) is a rough sketch of an actual piece of river, showing a number of different hazards (other rivers may have different hazards of course). You may think that it looks too difficult for you to tackle; nevertheless, it shows just the sort of place I would take people who could handle a canoe, who knew the basic strokes, and who were now ready for a little adventure. I would take them to this piece of upland river, and spend an hour or two in the pool below the rapid, teaching first the ferry glide, then the break in and break out. After that, I would run the rapid down, and then up and down, and so on for the rest of the time there. A trip on such a river would have to wait for another day.

But first, please check there isn't an angler just around the corner downstream, at the receiving end of the muddy water you may generate.

BREAK IN – BREAK OUT

The break in enables you to move out of the still water at

Figure 44. River section

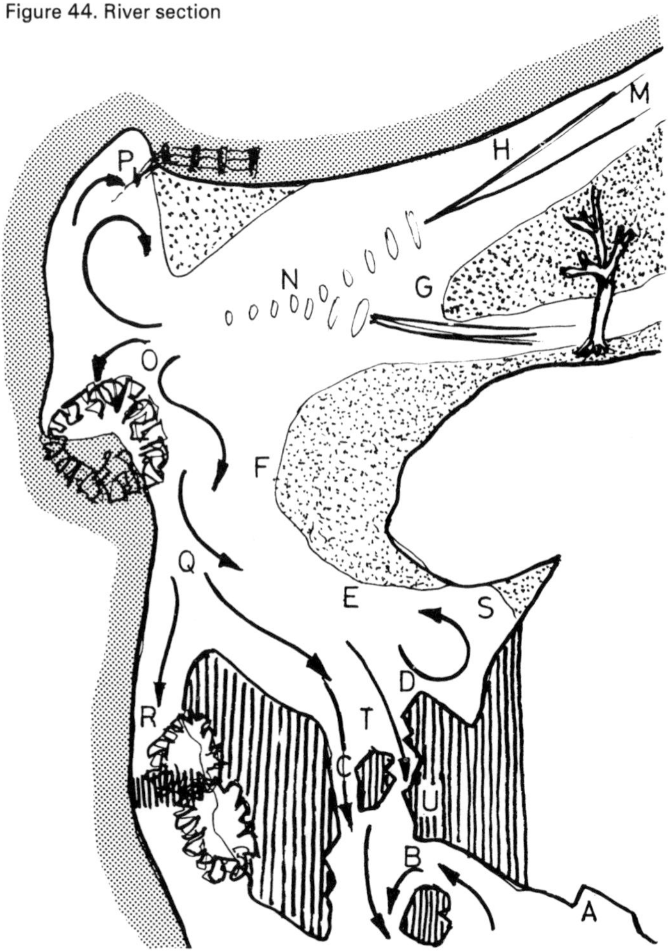

There are two ways to attempt this river: Start at 'A', bottom right corner; start at 'M' upper right corner. First, let's go upstream

A   Here the water is running towards B in an eddy. Gather speed and sprint to

B   Here you are paddling fast and meeting the fast downward flow of water, which will push you across to your left. You must necessarily go left of the rock in the middle. Here you go to

C   The water is running fast down between the rock in the middle and the rock at the side. Watch your paddle tips, or you may smash them against the rock, and try hard as you canoe up the 45 cm climb. As you emerge slowly above C the current will start to swing your bows across to the right to

D   Here the battle is mostly over, but you will need a rest. Go into the backwater S and watch the next paddler trying the climb. When you are ready, paddle steadily out via E and F avoiding the faster moving water. The stream will be shallow, with a pebble bottom: take care with your paddles

G   To get here you need to sprint again, and the two tail races from the streams will sweep you across to

H   Wait here and gain strength for the sprint across and up the next rapid. Once in the upstream pool you are ready to come down the section. You will have noted the fallen tree barring one way down the upper rapid, and the barbed wire fence at P

Now you go downstream

M   Keep to the middle of the flow. There seems to be an arrow of water and you should go down the middle of it. Avoid the rocks by using a draw stroke

N   Here you will find standing waves: a bit bumpy but fun. The confluence will cause a confused tumble of water. The currents start to swirl

O   At this point, you may have several choices. You can go back into the eddy at P and take a breather, or even swim with your upturned boat to the pebbly beach in order to empty out your canoe. However, such a spot is a trap for old branches, and a broken barbed wire fence may be trailing rusty strands in the water. Such strands can be very dangerous if they catch in your clothing

On the other hand, you may opt for the downriver trip, and the swirl or your own speed may take you under the bush or tree, where low branches can sweep you out of your cockpit. NEVER reach up to grab a branch for 'safety'. You will be wrenched out of your cockpit immediately as the current takes your boat away and you are left hanging under the bush. The branch bends, and drops you in the water. You cling on, naturally. The current sweeps you down and forward; the branch pulls you back and up. And so you start to oscillate, until good sense or weakness tells you to release your hold, when you will probably float free. But you could get caught up on underwater snags

Stay clear of overhangs

Q   All being well you have now reached this point. You have a choice. You can go right to R, and take the narrow way behind the island. You thus avoid the other paddlers still attempting to go up river. So to

R   You will take a sudden drop, perhaps. You will know you must go clear of the bushes on your left. However the old roots, from which the soil has been washed away, are a sort of wooden net in which your bows can latch up as they go out over the edge of the little fall, if you are a little too close to the bushes. You might not see that tangle if you approach too quickly, and the water is foaming

S   On the other hand, you might go across to this little haven, and wait until the rapid at T is unoccupied. You have a choice of two ways here, but at

U   There is an edge of rock which can catch your bows. You stop, and the back end of your canoe is swept across and crashes into the central rock. Your kayak then rolls over upstream and could be severely damaged

But it is fun. Do try. Don't let me put you off.   77

Figure 45. Break in; break out

the side of a river into the fast moving water in the middle of the river, without loss of balance. The break out enables you to do the reverse – move from the fast moving water to the still water.

The basic principle when meeting water coming towards you – ie when breaking in or out, when stuck on a rock in a steam, or when running down the face of a surfing wave, is to present the bottom of your canoe to the oncoming water. For an efficient break in, find a spout of water on a fast running stream, preferably where the power of the water is almost exhausted, where the main stream is slowing down after an easy rapid. Turn carefully into the faster water, bows first. Lean gently onto the downstream paddle, in a low telemark. Try and keep the centre of the boat, during the turn, over the boundary between the stream and the still water. If you are too far in you will do an S turn; if you're not far enough in, you won't turn into the faster moving water.

Improve your performance by breaking in from the left and the right sides, working higher up towards where the water is moving really fast. Be wary of the pull back on a weir, or a river stopper (see page 80). When you feel confident breaking in forwards, from both sides, start again at the easy end of the spout and try breaking in backwards, again from the left and right sides.

The break out is performed similarly, moving into the still water. Be careful that you don't spin as you turn, and end up back in the faster water again.

FERRY GLIDE

Ferry glide is the term used to describe a way a boat can be made to cross a river without going upstream or downstream. It's rather like the type of ferry which has a rope stretched from bank to bank above the water. A pulley runs freely on the rope, with a boat tethered to a rope attached to the pulley.

You don't have a cable with a pulley. Therefore to practice, find a piece of water running at about 3 to 5 km/h, and select a mark on each bank between which you wish to run. Imagine that there is a tight thread from one mark going in one of your ears, out of the other, and on to the far mark. Don't break the thread. Practice starting off from either bank, backwards as well as forwards.

The river has several rates of flow, usually with the fastest in the middle and the slowest at the edges. To make progress at a given speed – say half speed, you first

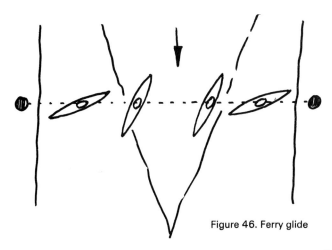

Figure 46. Ferry glide

head across the river to a point somewhere above the mark to which you want to go. As you leave the slow stream, angle further upstream as the flow of water becomes stronger (Figure 46). You will enter then the slower water on the other side of the river. Again, point your bows further across the stream, and you should arrive at the mark selected. You may make a mess of the action and be swept off downstream; if so, you simply start again.

Alternatively, try this move with a constant angle to the stream – ie by varying the speed of the canoe to cope with the different streams of water. Practice this move at the same time as you practice the break in and break out. Try turning the canoe using the different rates of water flow to help you.

STOPPER

This is where water has come down from upstream at some speed, and meets the still water below a fall, or rapid, or weir spill. The water in a stopper bounces upwards, and curls backwards, so that floating objects tend to be sent back upstream. A stopper, unlike a breaking wave at sea, doesn't change much from hour to hour, and remains in the same place. The only way through a stopper is to paddle 'like blazes' and keep on paddling.

WEIRS

There are two types of water gate on a weir: the butt gate and the radial gate. The butt gate is simply a movable part of the wall – ie the gate slides up a gantry fitted inside the wall, thus allowing the water to flow out under the gate. The radial gate is a section of a drum, and is hinged to swing upwards on transverse horizontal pivots. It is also counterbalanced for easy control.

The concrete abutments of the radial gate usually extend downstream several metres, thus providing a contained area of water with a fast moving undercurrent.

This piles the water up into a standing wave at the mouth of the downstream abutments, where the surface water flows back towards the radial gate. The area inside the standing wave is very, very dangerous, as floating objects tend to be tossed about inside the area, until they are smashed.

Some weirs have side retaining walls each side of the outflowing water, and a powerful surface return flow is to be expected. Sometimes an underwater ridge will throw the surface water back towards the gate. If you are going to play around in this sort of area, study the weir first. Watch the surface flow just under the weir; if the return flow extends for more than half a metre, it could prove dangerous.

Curved or horseshoe weirs with an arched formation, the crown of the arch being directed upstream, have a nasty habit of collecting debris or anything floating in the centre of the hollow of the arch. This is not a good place to be, if you have to swim wearing a lifejacket, or if your canoe is waterlogged.

F

Bristol Channel. The waves are breaking twice — far out, the wave height is about $3\frac{1}{2}$ m. The spray shows that a strong breeze is blowing. A canoe-wrecking scene

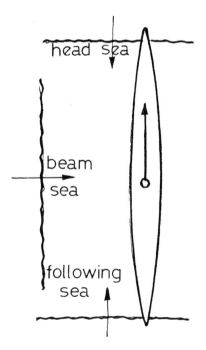

Figure 48. Head, beam and following sea

10 The Sea

SEA CANOEING/KAYAKING

The sea is fascinating, but it is dangerous, and powerful; and can prove fatal, if you're not careful. The best advice I can offer is – don't go alone; always go with someone who has been to sea before, and who knows the sea. Always plan any trips, however short, very carefully, and remember to check the weather reports before you set off.

It will take you at least six months even to start to learn the mysteries of the sea, and to develop the respect which it demands. There is much to be read about sea canoeing, and the book list (page 94) suggests two books which give reliable advice.

Figure 47 (page 84), a sketch of a beach and headland, has much to tell about specific conditions which can be met there. The best way to weigh up a beach and its potential is to see it at low tide and at high tide, and to relate the information so obtained to that found in the tide tables.

HEAD, BEAM AND FOLLOWING SEA

Figure 48 (opposite) shows a canoe and its relationship to the three main types of wave. These waves are known as the 'sea', which word is used here to describe a condition rather than a place.

If you are in difficulty, it is easiest to cope with a head sea. The ride is wet and lively, and exciting, and demands a fighting response, but it is not likely to cause motion sickness, as you can see the 'sea' coming towards you. The following sea is unpleasant, but you can make faster progress. The ride is always uneasy, a sort of

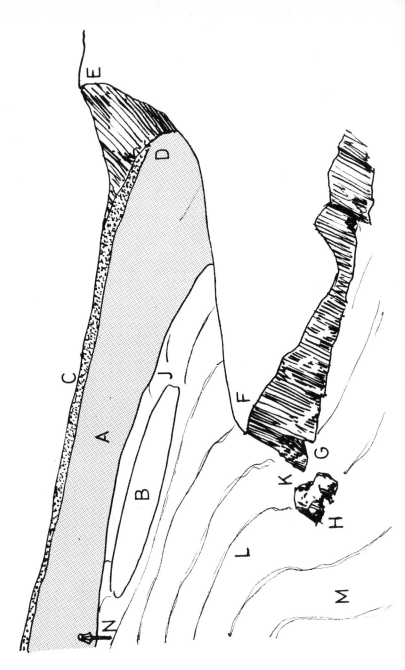

Figure 47. Headland and bay

A   The sand beach, where novice sea canoeists would mostly find themselves. The tides will reach different points on the beach on different days and at different times. The beach slopes gently down from the rocks at the back to the water's edge and beyond

B   The sand bank, which becomes visible as the tide goes down. The water must then flow away to the sides in the rip channel, J. The sandbank may only show at low water spring tides, but its effect will be felt at low tide

C   The storm beach, where large rocks and boulders are piled up at high spring tides. You may end up surfing amongst these at high tide, which can be very damaging to your canoe

D   An area of fallen rocks from the loose cliff face above. Don't pitch camp there, it would be asking for trouble. If the rocks are raw and sharp edged, they may well have fallen from the cliffs not long ago

E   You can view the beach from here before canoeing. Stand back a couple of metres from the edge – it may crumble and you could end up on the rocks below

F   A headland, a suitable place for viewing the beach, and for viewing the tidal effects at K, L and M. View these at half tide, both springs and neaps, when the flow of the currents can best be assessed – ie could I paddle against them?

G   A cave, where you can go exploring by canoe. Fascinating, exciting, but dangerous without experienced companions

H   An offshore rock; great for playing around, and landing on if you can

J   The rip channel. The water will flow from behind it, as waves break over the sand bank, even before the sand bank begins to show. Do not try to swim directly into shore, but at an angle along it. Surfers will look for the rip channel where it carves a sandy swathe out to sea. This is the fast way out to the big surf: when you know what you are doing

K   The narrow strait between the cliff and the offshore rock. The sea swell will surge through here, and the waves can be high. Surfing may be possible here when the waves are too flat off the beach. Beware of colliding with the rocks, and remember that once through the strait there is no convenient place to go. If the tidal current is from left to right, a swimmer will be washed away along the cliff coast where there are difficult exit problems

L   Bay currents are generated by the passage of the main tide across the mouth of the bay. There is no way of knowing which way the bay current may flow without watching it

M   Where the tide race will be; if the water is fast enough, and the bottom is shallow enough. Under water there is a ridge of rock, and the flow of the tide across it pushes up standing waves, and boiling surges

N   This basket indicates a sewerage outlet

85

swaying motion, which is likely to cause motion sickness to those sensitive to it. The canoe tends to run away downwave and to broach, or turn sideways, which can prove difficult. If the canoe is well under control, a following sea provides a very fast way to move, as the waves can be surfed and, to some extent, their energy can be used.

The beam, or side, sea is frustrating and unstable, and the crest (the top of the wave) affects the whole length of the canoe, sometimes tipping it over. The best way to approach this sea is in a series of swerves; angle the bows through the crest, then run parallel in the trough (the bottom of the wave).

Translate the 'sea' into the wind. A head wind slows you down, and blows spray into your face. A stern wind tends to turn the canoe. A side wind accentuates the turning qualities of your boat, and all but the most well balanced of boats will tend to turn head to wind – constantly, wearingly, frustratingly. A rudder or skeg attached to your boat will help just about to eradicate this side effect.

The wind against the sea means trouble: a constant short and choppy sea, with breaking crests. The wind with the sea means a building sea, with the waves becoming increasingly bigger. The wind across the sea, means that the sea develops a chop on the back of a swell.

TRANSIT

When you go to sea, you may want to go out around the headland, and see what is in the next bay. Why not? Provided you know that there isn't going to be a great tide race thrashing the water to foam just out of sight around the corner, with no way out up a vertical cliff.

Off you go, and you paddle and drift, and look about and paddle some more. When you are out at sea, and more than say $\frac{1}{4}$ km from some fixed point, it is difficult to know which way the tides are taking you. This is when a knowledge of, and how to observe, transits is very useful.

You are out at sea – look along the coast and line up a distant mark with a near one. It may be that a distant white farmhouse on a hill 6 km away lines up with a distinctively-shaped rock across the bay, perhaps $\frac{1}{2}$ km away. The farmhouse is directly over the rock from where you are sitting. If you paddle across the little bay towards the rock, keeping the two marks in line, and the bows of the canoe pointing along that line, it is clear that there is no sideways current. When tides run fast, as they do for example in the Bristol Channel, currents may be present. Then you might keep the canoe on its chosen line only by angling the bows up to 45° away from the chosen line. In that case, half your effort is used to make forward progress, and half in correcting a powerful sideways drift.

If you wish simply to observe a coastal drift, stop paddling and come to rest on the water. Look at the coast nearby. Line up an object on the foreshore with an object on a hill behind. If the rear object is moving right to left (say), relative to the forward object, then that is the direction of drift also, and a rough estimate of its speed can be made, by judging whether the two objects move away from each other slowly or quickly. Experience will help you judge the approximate speed of drift.

SURFING

Going Afloat on the Sea Put the canoe in shallow water, say 7 or 10 cm. Step in; the canoe should rest on the bottom. Make yourself comfortable, then wait until a small wave surges up around the boat and use the paddle shaft as a rpop, and your knuckles on the other side, to hitch the canoe inch by inch into deeper water. As soon as you feel that the canoe is fully afloat, wait until the next little wave comes up and then you will have sufficient depth to get your paddle into the water and start heading out. You will need to go afloat in water where there are no obstructions – such as breakwaters, swimmers, little children paddling, or other surfers.

First Drill Lay the canoe sideways to the small, 60 cm-high, broken waves coming inshore. As the wave is about to collide with the side of the canoe, lean right into the wave with an outstretched flat blade. Don't look at the wave, but watch where you are going (Figure 49). As the wave slaps into your side, you will feel as if you are being rolled over towards the shore. Resist this by leaning on the paddle shaft. If you don't do this . . . well, the water's only knee deep, and you can start again.

Second Drill Paddle sideways across the face of the waves, and as each smacks into the boat, you will find you can handle the canoe by paddling straight through them (Figure 50). If you don't paddle through forcefully, you will be sent in sideways towards the beach and the smaller waves. Soon, however, you will find you are going so far out that the waves are much bigger, and you are swept in sideways whatever you do. Having learned how to handle a broached kayak, you can now try and get out into the green waves.

Third Drill Head straight into the waves. Your left forearm is right across your face (Figure 51), to break the force of the breaking wave, which smacks into your face and squirts water up your nose with great power. This is unpleasant; so brace through the wave, head down into the crook of your elbow, and keep on paddling until you are out beyond the break.

Once you are on the unbroken waves beyond the break, you must look out all around you for other surfers, and for swimmers and surfboard riders. The break line of the waves moves all the time, but eventually you must start to move in. If you have selected the conditions correctly, the waves won't be bigger than 1 m or so, and you can have a lot of fun based on what you have learned already. However, one day you will feel the bows dip down and down, the wave will break and you will be hurled over into a loop (Figure 52). You will have time to recognise what is happening to you. Try to reach a blade down into the water on one side or the other, and the

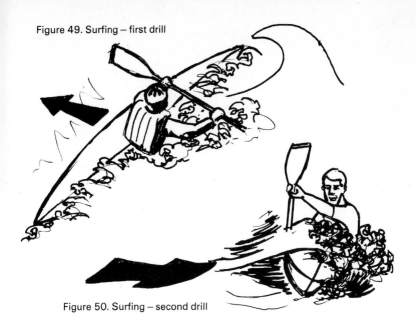

Figure 49. Surfing – first drill

Figure 50. Surfing – second drill

Figure 51. Surfing – third drill

Figure 52. Surfing – loop and spin out

blade's leverage might just spin you round in a half roll as you finish your half loop. This is the loop and spin out, and leaves you the right way up, facing the opposite way, whizzing in backwards. The full loop involves going right over twice. Very often the loop requires a roll after the loop. When rolling, *always* roll down towards the shore and up on the wave side.

DUMPERS

Dumpers are destructive waves, which are found on steeply shelving shores, where they suddenly rise up, crest, break and fall in a welter of roaring water, which is often discoloured by the shingle and sand pulled up from the bottom. They travel hardly any distance and then surge back – the undertow – and undercut the next wave coming in to the shore.

Keep out of dumpers – they release their energy in two seconds of destructive collapse.

11 Sport

Canoe sport embraces a wide range of games and competitions, and there isn't space in this book to cover all its aspects. Slalom is perhaps the best known, and requires the most skill – precision timing and a good knowledge of *all* the strokes. Long distance and sprint racing are also very popular, once you have learnt the basics. There are several games which can be played, even whilst you are still learning, and indeed they will help you understand the way a canoe moves and how it can be moved. Canoe polo and wiggle/wriggle are two such games, although the details given must necessarily be brief.

CANOE POLO

Canoe polo is played five a side, seven minutes each way, with a plastic no 5 size football. The goals are targets 1 m square, with the lower edges set 2 m above the water. The targets must face each other, and be not less than 20 m and not more than 30 m apart. The pitch can be any area of water that allows the proper spacing of the targets. The canoes must be between 2–3 m long, and between 0.5–0.6 m beam. The canoe ends must be rounded, not less than 10 cm radius in plan, and not less than 5 cm radius in profile. The paddlers must wear helmets, and body padding to protect the kidneys, spleen etc.

The rules are available from the British Canoe Union, and the National Final takes place in February each year at the canoeing exhibition at Crystal Palace.

WIGGLE/WRIGGLE

The wiggle/wriggle can be played with any canoe, but particularly with slalom kayaks. A simple slalom gate is set up on still water, usually a swimming pool. The paddler sits ready to enter the centre of the gate and, when the timekeeper is ready, enters it and then uses the gate to do nine different 'gates' against the clock. Timing starts as the bows break the gate line on the way in, and ends when the bow slides out at the end. The sequence of gates is as follows:

1 Forward through. Right about turn.
2 Forward through. Left about turn.
3 Forward through. Reverse past right. R
4 Forward through. Reverse past left. R
5 Forward through. Reverse past left again.
6 Right about reverse turn. Reverse through.
7 Left about reverse turn. Reverse through. R
8 Forward past right. Reverse through. R
9 Forward past left. Reverse through.

(Right about means with your right shoulder to the gate. Left about means with your left shoulder to the gate.)

A touch disqualifies. Novices find it less difficult if touches are allowed, but these are charged at the rate of ten seconds for each touch of the gate poles. Novices might score upwards of 300 on their first attempt; experts get through in less than 60 seconds with no faults. The wriggle competition includes a roll at each of the points marked R in the above instructions. Each roll takes about two seconds.

12 Useful Information

ORGANISATIONS

British Canoe Union
    70 Brompton Road
    London SW3 1DT

Facilities are available for individual, family and club
membership. The various technical committees com-
prise: Touring, Coaching, Sprint, Long Distance,
Sailing, Polo, Sea and Surf.

British Schools' Canoeing Association
Sec: J E Saunders
    New Farmhouse
    77 Melton Road
    Loughborough
    Leicestershire LE12 5AG

Governing body of schools' canoeing associations.

Surf Lifesaving Association of Great Britain
Sec: Alan Goodwin
    4 Cathedral Yard
    Exeter
    Devon EX1 1HG

Governing body of surf lifesaving groups in Britain.

National Coastal Rescue Training Centre
    Commander Charles Thomson
    Aberavon Lido
    Port Talbot
    South Wales

Courses are available for all types of organised groups in
surf rescue using canoes, inshore rescue craft, surf skis,
reel and line etc.

THE TRADE

The supply of canoes, kayaks etc is complicated; you can buy new canoes cheaper than you can buy second hand ones. You must take advice if you do not know the market. The BCU trade list is fairly comprehensive, and is available from the address given on the previous page.

The trade itself has its own governing body, which does take care that its members are producing reliable craft. So, if you want an implied certificate of quality, buy a canoe from a firm listed by the British Canoe Manufacturers Association, 'Avoncraft', Burrowfield, Welwyn Garden City, Herts. Their mark is on all the canoes produced by members.

The best place to see all the boats, equipment and books is to visit the annual canoeing exhibition, held at Crystal Palace, London in February each year.

BOOK LIST

The BCU publishes a series of booklets about the sport, some of which are very good, and they are not expensive.

The following books are recommended for further reading, as are the canoeing magazines.

Living Canoeing by Alan Byde (A & C Black).
Beginners' Guide to Canoeing by Alan Byde (Pelham).
Canoe Building in Glass-Reinforced Plastic by Alan Byde (A & C Black).
Canoe Design and Construction by Alan Byde (Pelham).
Sea Canoeing by Derek Hutchinson (A & C Black).
Canoeing Complete edited by Brian Skilling (Kaye and Ward). Contains ten chapters written by experts in their field, and has a comprehensive bibliography.

Canoeing in Britain (Ocean Publications Ltd). Six issues per year.
Canoeing Magazine (Canoeing Press). Monthly.
Canoe Focus. Free to members of BCU.

Glossary

BEAM. Widest part of a canoe.

BLADE. Small spade-like piece at one or each end of a paddle shaft. Also the turning part of a rudder.

BOW RUDDER. A stroke that turns the canoe whilst it is moving.

BREAK IN/BREAK OUT (In USA, CUT IN/CUT OUT.). Break-in is moving from still water in a river into the fast moving stream; the converse is a break-out.

BROACHED. Laid sideways to the sea. Parallel to the wave crest.

BULKHEAD. Partition; division between one part of the hull and another.

CAPSIZE. To turn upside down when afloat in a canoe.

COCKPIT. The hollowed out section in the middle of the deck, in which the paddler sits.

DECK. The top part of the canoe.

DRAW STROKE. A stroke that moves the canoe sideways.

DUMPER. A short, sudden, destructive wave-break, right on the shore.

FEATHER. When one paddle blade is set at right angles to the other, which reduces wind resistance on the upper blade when paddling.

FERRY GLIDE. A method of crossing a river without the boat going upstream or downstream.

FOOTREST. A cross bar inside the canoe, against which you press your feet.

GUNWALE. The joint between the deck and the hull.

HANDED. If right handed, use blades which are feathered so that they are handed on the right, and vice versa.

HIGH TELEMARK. An advanced stroke used mainly in slalom and for breaking out.

HIP FLICK. To twist the body to release effort explosively. Used in rolling.

HULL. The bottom part of the canoe.

KEEL. The bottom part of the hull.

LOA. Length overall; length of boat excluding the rudder.

LOW TELEMARK. A stroke that turns the canoe and slows it down.

PADDLE. Single bladed or double bladed. Primarily used as a lever by which you move your craft about in the water.

PADDLE PARK. A piece of elastic stretched from side to side in front of the cockpit, under which can be stowed paddles and loose gear.

RAFTING. A method of enabling several canoeists to link up together.

ROCKER. The upward curvature of the keel towards the ends of a canoe.

ROLLING. A method of capsizing, remaining in the cockpit, and 'rolling' up to the surface on the opposite side to that on which you capsized. A method of self rescue, and an essential skill in surfing.

RUDDER. A blade fixed to the under rear of the hull, which can be controlled by the paddler so that the canoe can be turned or kept straight.

SCULLING. Using the paddle blade rhythmically to deflect water, and so move the canoe in the desired direction.

SHAFT. The handle of the paddle, to which is joined the blade(s).

SKEG. A fixed rudder used to keep the craft straight.

SPLICING. A method of securing a fastening; ie 3 strand line is woven into itself, either end to end or in an eye.

SPRAY DECK. A separate flexible extension of the deck, which seals around the paddler and prevents water from entering the cockpit.

STARBOARD BOW. In front on the right.

STERN RUDDER. A stroke that turns the canoe to the left or right whilst it is slowing down.

STOPPER. A riverine dumper; a dangerous wave of standing water.

SUPPORT STROKE. An advanced form of the draw stroke.

SURFING. To canoe on the wave crests as they roll in and break on the shore.

SURF SKI. A sort of surfboard with an open cockpit, in which the paddler sits.

SWEEP TURN. A stroke that turns the boat either when it's stationary or when it's moving.

TRANSIT. A method of estimating tidal drifts, and to keep a course in good visibility.